Gender and Corporate Boards

The lack of women on boards has galvanised much public and policy interest, which has led to many countries introducing quotas for women on boards or to concerted voluntary action. However, the way that directors are appointed remains opaque and prone to the influence of gender.

Using a social constructionist understanding of gender and a discourse analysis, *Gender and Corporate Boards* explores the board appointment process through the experiences of women and men seeking non-executive board roles. The book is unique in that it traces board-ready candidates who have been vetted by an executive search firm over an 18-month period. By taking a longitudinal and prospective view rather than retrospective and snapshot, it provides deep analysis of how the board appointment process is gendered. This volume privileges the voices of those who are seeking board roles to show how they make sense of an unpredictable and complex process.

Gender and Corporate Boards first analyses how aspirant board candidates see themselves in relation to the market through exploring their perceptions of the ideal board member and how they position themselves towards this ideal. Second, the book shows how candidates must leverage their networks to get board appointments and that the process is gendered: women and men receive different benefits from their networks. Third, the book explores how the participants make sense of success and failure and how their justifications are also gendered.

The book will be of interest to those seeking to understand the dynamics of gender on boards, as well as those interested in gender and leadership more broadly.

Scarlett Brown is an independent researcher specialising in diversity, corporate governance, and business as a force for good in society.

Elisabeth Kelan is Professor of Leadership and Organisation at Essex Business School, University of Essex, United Kingdom.

Routledge Studies in Gender and Organizations
Series Editor: Elisabeth Kelan

Although still a fairly young field, the study of gender and organizations is increasingly popular and relevant. There are few areas of academic research that are as vibrant and dynamic as the study of gender and organizations. While much earlier research has focused on documenting the imbalances of women and men in organizations, more recently, research on gender and organizations has departed from counting men and women. Instead, research in this area sees gender as a process: something that is done rather than something that people are. This perspective is important and meaningful as it takes researchers away from essentialist notions of gender and opens the possibility of analysing the process of how individuals become women and men. This is called 'gendering', 'practising gender', 'doing gender' or 'performing gender' and draws on rich philosophical traditions.

Whilst Routledge Studies in Gender and Organizations has a broad remit, it will be thematically and theoretically committed to exploring gender and organizations from a constructivist perspective. Rather than focusing on specific areas of organizations, the series is to be kept deliberately broad to showcase the most innovative research in this field. It is anticipated that the books in this series will make a theoretical contribution to the field of gender and organization based on rigorous empirical explorations.

Gender, Age and Inequality in the Professions
Edited by Marta Choroszewicz and Tracey L. Adams

Judith Butler and Organization Theory
Melissa Tyler

Gender and Corporate Boards
The Route to a Seat at the Table
Scarlett Brown and Elisabeth Kelan

For a full list of titles in this series, please visit www.routledge.com

Gender and Corporate Boards

The Route to a Seat at the Table

Scarlett Brown and Elisabeth Kelan

Routledge
Taylor & Francis Group

LONDON AND NEW YORK

First published 2020 by Routledge

2 Park Square, Milton Park, Abingdon, Oxon OX14 4RN

605 Third Avenue, New York, NY 10017

Routledge is an imprint of the Taylor & Francis Group, an informa business

First issued in paperback 2021

Library of Congress Cataloging-in-Publication Data
A catalog record for this book has been requested

ISBN: 978-1-138-65244-6 (hbk)
ISBN: 978-1-03-217550-8 (pbk)
DOI: 10.4324/9781315624266

Typeset in Sabon
by Apex CoVantage, LLC

This book is dedicated to Scarlett's father, Peter Goodridge, whose support for this work was unwavering but who did not live to see it published.

Contents

Acknowledgements   viii
Foreword   x

1   Golden Times for Women on Boards?   1

2   Gender and Corporate Boards   6

3   The Ideal Board Member   24

4   The Art of Networking   53

5   Leaning In and Sitting Back   81

6   Gender and the Pathway to the Boardroom   109

Appendices   129
References   130
Index   144

Acknowledgements

In December 2011, Kate Grussing and Elisabeth Kelan attended a lecture by Madeleine Albright at the London School of Economics and Political Science. If memory serves well, Madeleine Albright did mention her famous quote 'there is a special place in hell for women who don't help other women' (Albright, 2016) during that event. Little did Kate and Elisabeth realise that this meeting would become the starting point for a long-term research project in which this quote would be referred to. We discussed whether, in spite of the focus on women on boards, it still takes women longer to secure a seat at the board table. Elisabeth developed a research proposal that was funded by the Economic and Social Research Council through a collaborative studentship with Kate's firm, Sapphire Partners, at King's College London. Scarlett Brown was awarded this studentship and conducted the interviews and the analysis. Scarlett then wrote her PhD thesis based on the material, which subsequently became this book.

Jonathan Hindmarsh's advice was indispensable in setting up the project and during the project itself. Without his support and guidance, it is unlikely that this book would exist. Rosalind Gill provided advice on the project from the beginning, and we are grateful for all her support throughout the process. Aditi Gupta served on the PhD supervisory team, providing both her expertise on boards and her supportive attitude. Scarlett's PhD was examined by Stephanie Taylor and Cathrine Seierstad, and the generosity in engaging with the material was immensely helpful in creating deeper and more nuanced interpretations.

Many people supported this project throughout the process. In particular, we would like to acknowledge the support of Sally Springbett, Anne Laure Humbert, Coni Judge and Caroline Carter. Scarlett would like to thank her mum, Melanie, her partner, James, for his support in helping to finish the book, and Emily, Elle, and Tessa, without whom the PhD would never have been completed.

We would also like to thank the team at Routledge, particularly Brianna Ascher and Mary Del Plato, for their support throughout this process.

The research would not be possible without the support of our interviewees. We are grateful for your time and your openness about this otherwise rather opaque process.

Our gratitude goes to Kate Grussing for being a champion of women in the workplace and making this project possible in the first place.

Some parts of the material have been published in other formats:

- Brown, S.E. (2016). PhD Barbie Gets a Makeover! Aesthetic Labour in Academia, in Elias, A.S., Gill, R., Scharff, C. (eds.), *Aesthetic Labour: Rethinking Beauty Politics in Neoliberalism*, Basingstoke: Palgrave Macmillan, 149–163.
- Brown, S.E., & Kelan, E. (2016). 'There's Never Been a Better Time to be a Woman?: The Discursive Effects of Women on Boards Research Reports'. In Elliot, C., Stead., V., Mavin, S., and Williams, J., (eds.) *Gender, Media, and Organization: Challenging Mis(s) Representations of women Leaders and Management*, Charlotte NC: Information Age Publishing, 77–95.
- Brown, S.E., Kelan, E.K., Humbert, A.L. (2015). *Opening the Black Box: Comparing Women's and Men's Routes to the Boardroom.* Retrieved from https://www.dropbox.com/s/syhsdx64hqtcw4w/ Opening%20The%20Black%20Box.pdf?dl=0.

Foreword

For decades, the progress of women into corporate boardrooms has been assiduously tracked, but their individual journeys through the labyrinth were more akin to a big black box. Professor Kelan and Dr Brown have taken on this puzzle with painstaking rigour and applied their insight and intellect into dissecting the different paths of men and women in order to guide future generations of board members. When I first suggested to Professor Kelan my intellectual curiosity (borne from years as a headhunter) into systematically dissecting what lay behind the successful candidates versus their peers, she was instantly excited by the research question and could see that this research had the potential to shed new light on the opaque career path while also identifying what was gendered in the experience.

The detailed research was a true partnership between the researchers, my colleagues and myself at Sapphire Partners and our female and male research subjects who opened up their professional aspirations and actions to scrutiny. This research delves deeper and looks under the proverbial car bonnet, and it merits attention from aspiring board members, board governance champions and enlightened chairmen and chairwomen, as well as executive search consultants and headhunters.

The research follows the often-circuitous search pathways of high-potential board candidates, male and female, and by taking a longitudinal approach, it carries greater weight than peer studies that take a single point-in-time approach. For Professor Kelan and Dr Brown, this research method required them to show enormous patience and diligence as they waited for the board candidates to pursue board appointments, which often can take months or years to come to fruition.

This paradox of how to crack into the ranks of corporate boardrooms is not an easy topic to empirically analyse, being prone to highly variable benchmarks for due process, extreme confidentiality, complex personalities, nuanced feedback, opaque networking affects, differing perceptions, hypersensitivity and high-performing executive egos. Our fearless academics were relentless in their pursuit of the 'secret sauce', and we were patient in our coaching of them on how boards and companies and the executive search process work in the real world.

I am confident that this research will assist the growth of more diverse boards by encouraging a more rigorous selection process by both board and executive search communities. I am also optimistic that more women and left-field men will persist and succeed in their searches for board roles—emboldened by the insights in this book. I am also hopeful that more chairs will appreciate the important role they have in encouraging and sponsoring first-time directors. The battle is not yet won, but the campaign is gaining momentum and rigour thanks to this overdue research.

In my day job leading executive search consultancy at Sapphire Partners, I'm constantly energised by the calibre of the candidates I meet. Fortunately, I'm also increasingly encouraged by the enlightened chairs and board directors who value greater professionalisation of the board appointment process as a fundamental building block for good corporate governance. The important role of ambitious and thoughtful academics like Professor Kelan and Dr Brown shining a spotlight on the labyrinth of corporate boards and their appointment processes cannot be underestimated. On behalf of so many aspiring board candidates, as well as my colleagues, I am grateful for the opportunity to have helped support, sponsor, shape and encourage this insightful research, which has helped to lift the veil on the board appointment process.

Kate Grussing
Managing Director and Founder
Sapphire Partners

1 Golden Times for Women on Boards?

Getting a seat at the board table has seemed a distant possibility for most women throughout history. Boardrooms have traditionally been dominated by an elite group of senior men, and women were absent from those boards. This started to change most notably when, in 2008, Norway became the first country to set a legal quota for women on boards. Across the world, there followed a flurry of activity to get more women on boards with or without some kind of quota or target. While the impetus and focus for women on boards seems to be generally well received, the approach of how to get women there diverged. Some countries, such as Norway, introduced a hard, legislative quota for women, while other countries, like the United Kingdom (UK), followed a voluntary approach, which was regarded as a collaboration between business and the government. This created a climate where it seemed almost a foregone conclusion that if you were a woman in a reasonably senior role, you would be sought to serve on a board.

In this book, we trace the pathways of women and men searching for their first board roles. Through longitudinal interviews, we illustrate the subjective experiences of how these board-ready women and men make sense of their search for board roles and of their successes and failures to become directors. We shed light on how the right experience, personality and fit are discursively constructed, we show how strategic, yet subtle, networking is seen as essential to attain a board role, and we show how women lean in while men sit back on their journey to the boardroom. Overall, the book makes a contribution to understanding how aspiring board members make sense of the board appointment process in a climate where, publicly, there was emphasis on appointing more women to boards of directors.

Women on Boards—An Apparent Success Story

The focus on women on boards is often constructed as a success story. Following from Norway's initial quota for women on boards, a wave of similar initiatives emerged. Some countries followed the Norway model of mandatory quotas for women on boards with sanctions (Wang and Kelan, 2013) while others used a softer approach to quotas without sanctions, such as in Spain, India and Malaysia (Kirsch, 2018). Yet others focused on voluntary action rather than mandatory quotas, such as in the UK. The UK's approach featured a governmental review (the 'Davies Review'), setting a target of 25% women on boards for the Financial Times Stock Exchange (FTSE) 100, with five years to achieve it. The UK's focus on women on boards predated 'Brexit', the UK's expected departure from the European Union (EU) after the 2016 referendum; this is ironic given that the UK's action was driven by the threat of potential quotas being enshrined in an EU directive. At the point of writing, such a directive has not been introduced (Humbert *et al.*, 2019).

While the increase of women on boards globally is rightly celebrated as a success, success has many fathers (and mothers), and many stakeholders claim credit for this achievement. Of course, all had a stake in pushing for change—legislators, regulators, business leaders and politicians—and the 'women on boards' campaign was notable for being spearheaded by women in leadership roles. Either way, it appears that the time was right to focus on getting women onto boards, and the change took place in a specific historic, social and political context. In the UK, the voluntary approach taken is often told as a success story that demonstrates that businesses can get more women into senior roles through a voluntary commitment if they just try hard enough.

The focus of women on boards at this time also exists in a wider context: it was constructed as a golden age for women in leadership. The media regularly ran stories about how women were wanted on boards and that board diversity was changing rapidly. The market responded: there sprung up a range of networking events and courses offered to women who aspire to board positions. Search firms were asked to locate women who can sit on boards. This led to the impression for many women that they just had to put themselves forward to get a board seat. Motivational books like *Lean In* (Sandberg, 2013) published around the time also espoused that if women can just have a bit more confidence, they could be successful. At the time, the possibility of portfolio careers, which afford individuals the opportunity to design their own work context by combining different projects, was also gaining prominence; board roles are quintessential examples of portfolio careers. Portfolio careers are constructed as particularly attractive for women because it allows them to schedule time for care work and leisure activities, which are often difficult to achieve in regular work structures, although research has questioned that optimistic view (Gill, 2002). Board roles, therefore, became an option that many women aspired to and invested substantially into developing themselves into board-ready candidates through attending courses and networking events. Simultaneously, the focus on women meant it appeared as though men would now struggle to get onto boards with women as new competition. Despite the belief that it was a good time to be a woman if one wants to get a seat at the boardroom table, recent figures suggest that 65% of all new appointments go to men and only 35% to women (Hampton and Alexander, 2018).

The success story of women on boards in the UK is made more complicated by two other key concerns. First, the progress made was largely in relation to non-executive directors. While the percentage of women in non-executive roles in FTSE 100 companies has increased from 15.6% in 2011 to 36.5% in 2018, the proportion of women in senior executive roles on boards has increased from 5.5% to 10.2% and remains low (Hampton and Alexander, 2018). This is understandable in such a short space of time: non-executive directors are part-time roles given to people external to the company; there is relatively regular turnover,[1] and there is no fixed requirement on how many non-executives a board can have. As such, changing the gender balance can be done fairly simply: by adding one or two women into non-executive director roles. This is demonstrably easier than increasing the number of women in high-level executive positions, as typically only the chief executive officer (CEO) and chief financial officer (CFO) sit on the boards. In 2018, only six women were CEOs of FTSE 100 companies (Hampton and Alexander, 2018). Since 2015, the *Hampton Alexander Review* (2018) has focused on this issue through encouraging companies to declare their gender balance of executive committees (one level below the board) and in senior management.

A second issue with the women-on-boards agenda that is less frequently discussed lies in our understanding of how non-executive directors are found, appraised and chosen by boards. In 2011, at the time the Davies' review was launched, it was suggested within the review that the appointment process is opaque, difficult to navigate and reliant on networks and that this contributes to the lack of women (Doldor *et al.*, 2012). The Davies' review, therefore, recommended that the process be made more rigorous, with the assumption that this would lead to more women being appointed (Davies, 2011, 2015). When the target was met in 2015, the question of whether the appointment process had become more rigorous was not raised. There is surprisingly little academic research that focuses on the board appointment perspective. When focusing on gender, research has tended to examine women directors, those who have 'made it', and therefore tends to be dominated either by demographic analysis of those women directors or on how appointing women can have an effect on the board or the company.

The Research

In a climate where there was a strong demand for more women on boards, it was assumed by many that it would be relatively easy for women to get board positions. At the same time, anecdotal evidence suggested that it still took women longer to get a board position than men and that the process was more difficult, while a great deal of academic research suggested that there was still bias towards men. This contradiction was at the heart of the research that forms the basis for this book. In order to shed light on the gender dimension of the appointment process, we designed a qualitative, in-depth and longitudinal study to help us understand the subjective experiences of women and men on the way to their first board roles.

As we were interested in the process, the study was longitudinal, interviewing aspiring board members three times while they were seeking board roles. The approach was prospective to ensure that we did not simply replicate the research that looks at women who have made it onto boards but rather looks at individuals who had a realistic chance of being board members as they were trying to get access to roles. This was supported by an executive search firm, Sapphire Partners, which has a lot of experience in both gender and board appointments.

The research followed the experiences of 30 aspirant directors, 15 men and 15 women, by interviewing them three times over a period of two years. The interviewees were all people who, by their own admission, were seeking to gain a non-executive director role on a FTSE 350 board. They came from a range of industry backgrounds, and the majority were based in London, UK. They were aged between 40 and 70 years old and all were white. The interviews were held in a variety of places in London, with some interviews conducted over the phone. With the interviewees permission, the interviews were all audio recorded. They were then fully transcribed and analysed.

The research approach was social constructionist in that we were interested in how gender is constructed in the board appointment process. We, therefore, used a discourse analysis to analyse the interviews. Discourse analysis is the search for patterns in language in the form of 'common sense' structures or interpretive repertoires (Edley, 2001; Wetherell, 1998) and examining language 'as used' (Taylor, 2001): the commonality of patterns and their discursive function and effect. This was done first by hand and then later using qualitative data analysis software. From this analysis, and our analysis of the literature, there emerged three key areas of focus. First, it became clear that there was a narrow perspective on what makes an 'ideal' board member, and that this is restrictive to diverse candidates. Second, we found that networking was seen as an essential part of the process but that the social expectations around what constitutes 'acceptable' networking excludes those who are not already in the right network. These expectations are also gendered and disadvantage women. Third, we found that the women-on-boards agenda engendered a belief that men were no longer being chosen, while, during that time, nearly three-quarters of roles still went to men. As well as illuminating the appointment process and how it is exclusionary to diversity, this research also demonstrates the importance of taking a broader perspective on gender and moving away from a conception that is solely focused on which bodies occupy a certain role.

Structure of the Book

The book is structured as follows. In Chapter 2, we outline the current research on women on boards to provide an understanding framework for this research and what is already known about directors, how they are appointed and what explanations have been used until now to explain women's absence. In Chapter 3, we then discuss the findings from this research, showing how the ideal director is conceptualised and how that concept is gendered. Chapter 4 focuses on networking practices to examine how women are included and excluded. In Chapter 5, we consider the wider views candidates have about the process and how these views have discursive effects: women are expected to push forward or 'lean in' to get roles while men sit back, while men and women alike believe that it is easier for women. The sixth chapter offers a summary and conclusion by demonstrating how a gendered view of the appointment process is essential to understand the board appointment process fully.

Conclusion

The topic of women on boards has garnered a lot of media, practitioner and academic interest in recent years. The scarcity of women on boards is often lamented, but some countries and regions have started to take proactive action in the form of quotas or voluntary commitments. This creates the impression that there is a lot of demand for women, but it also encourages supply by signalling to women that a board position is just within reach. In this book, we look at the board appointment process from the perspective of aspiring board candidates to explore the subjective experiences of women and men who seek a board appointment. Thereby we aim to reduce the opacity of board appointment processes and shed new light on the gender-board relationship.

Note

1. Non-executives on FTSE 100 boards are deemed non-independent after nine years and rarely stay on after this time period has lapsed.

2   Gender and Corporate Boards

Over recent decades, gender on corporate boards of directors has attracted significant scholarly interest, and it is thus not surprising that there is a plethora of academic articles and books that have been published on the topic. An excellent summary is provided by Kirsch (2018) in her systematic review of the field, which outlines how extant research falls into four main areas. First, scholars have analysed whether women on boards are different from men on boards. Second, research tries to understand those factors that shape women's appointments to boards and board gender composition. Third, researchers have analysed how women on boards affect organisational outcomes both internal and external. Fourth, research has explored the relationship between regulation and board diversity. Our research falls within the second stream, and we focus particularly on micro-level aspects in that our analysis centred on the search for board roles and the appointment process. Our interest is thus on social processes as they relate to board appointments. In particular, we focus on areas around human capital, the skills directors need to be on boards, the notion of fit and the importance of visibility and networking as part of the board appointment process. Our review of the literature is thus selective rather than exhaustive; we focus on aspects of the literature that connect to the analysis of the interview material. In particular, we suggest that research on gender and boards has paid insufficient attention to the sense-making practices of women and men on their journey to the boardroom.

Why So Few?

Being a director of a company is often seen as the crowning achievement for corporate leaders (Stern and Westphal, 2010; Sheridan *et al.*, 2015). Boards or 'boards of directors' are a group of individuals who work at the top of organisations. Here we have focused on corporate boards—boards of companies—but boards are also required on charities and other kinds of non-profit organisation. Boards' make-up, structure, role and responsibilities varies from country to country according to national regulation and business law, but they can be broadly understood as a group of individuals who are collectively responsible for the long-term success of the company (Financial Reporting Council, 2018: p. 7). Some countries, such as Germany, have dual board structures with a management board and a supervisory board. In a unitary board structure, such as the UK, a board has two to four executive directors (Lowe *et al.*, 2017), most commonly the CEO and CFO, and an equal or greater number of 'non-executive' or independent directors[1] who are responsible for monitoring the behaviour and decision making of the executive directors. Executive roles are full-time positions often taken by individuals who have worked up through a company or moved laterally from another, while non-executive roles are part-time (typically 10–40 days a year), and the nature of the work is focused largely around board meetings. Individuals will often hold more than one role on a number of boards or may hold a non-executive role alongside a full-time career.

Across the globe, women hold 17.3% of all directorships, and it is estimated that it will take at least until 2028 before women hold 30% of all directorships[2] (Eastman, 2017). The absence of women on corporate boards of directors has been highlighted as a key issue in the last two decades: in academic literature, media reports and wider societal discourse (see, for example, Aluchna and Aras, 2018; De Anca and Gabaldon, 2014; Fagan *et al.*, 2012; Devnew, 2018; Post and Byron, 2014; Seierstad and Opsahl, 2011; Seierstad *et al.*, 2017; Torchia *et al.*, 2011). The relatively small number of women in these roles is widely regarded as an issue that businesses and countries need to address, both from a utilitarian perspective and a social justice perspective. The utilitarian perspective suggests that the lack of women on boards is an issue because there is a 'business case' for women directors; women are an untapped pool of potential talent that can improve the way the board or company functions, either through their own contribution or through increasing the diversity of boards and reducing the likelihood of groupthink (Nielsen and Huse, 2010; Seierstad *et al.*, 2017; Seierstad, 2016). Independence is seen as important for a board to be effective, and as such, policymakers and governance scholars have pointed to the value of casting the net wider when recruiting directors and to increase to number of women (Adams, 2016). Another utilitarian argument falls into the third stream identified by Kirsch (2018): research that seeks to demonstrate that women directors have an impact on the organisations they join. A social justice perspective by contrast criticises the lack of women on boards due to it being representative of an imbalance of power. As boards represent highly powerful roles both within their organisations and in wider society, the lack of women on boards must be addressed on grounds of social fairness and equality (Seierstad *et al.*, 2017).

Across the world, there have been differing approaches to addressing this issue with policy, legislation and encouragement. In 2008, Norway became the first country to introduce a gender quota, requiring boards of companies over a certain size to have at least 40% of either sex on their boards. Since then, many other countries have followed suit (Adams, 2016; Eastman, 2017; Seierstad, 2016). The European Commission has submitted a proposal for a directive which was backed by the European Parliament, but eight national parliaments (Denmark, Poland, the Netherlands, the UK, Sweden and one of the two chambers of the Parliament of the Czech Republic) resisted the draft directive on the grounds of subsidiarity (European Parliament, 2019).

The UK, rejecting the notion of a legislated quota, took a business-led, 'collaborative' approach (Seierstad and Opsahl, 2011): a collaboration between the government, business leaders, professional services and search firms, academia and businesses resulted in a collective commitment to address the lack of women on boards. In 2011, the government produced the first 'Women on Boards' report (Davies, 2011)—the Davies' review—that set a target for 25% women on FTSE 100 boards by 2015. The combined efforts of corporate institutional and individual actors, state encouragement and pressure from the media (Seierstad *et al.*, 2017) saw the number of women on FTSE 100 boards rise from 12.5% in 2011 to 25% in 2015 (Seierstad *et al.*, 2017), meeting Lord Davies' target. Since 2015, there has been considerable effort to continue the momentum through, amongst other things, the *Hampton Alexander Review* (2018): a similar initiative that extended the target to 30% to companies outside the FTSE 100 and looks at women in senior roles below the board.

The Research Field of Women on Boards

Much research on women on boards has primarily looked at the impact women directors have on board effectiveness and company success (Ahern and Dittmar, 2012; Bear *et al.*, 2010; Biggins, 1999; Brammer *et al.*, 2009; Huse, 2008; Matsa and Miller, 2013; Sheridan *et al.*, 2011; Wang and Kelan, 2013) or at the characteristics and experiences of women directors (Bilimoria, 2000; Burgess and Theranou, 2002; Burke, 2000; Singh and Vinnicombe, 2004). The former often stems from a desire to make a 'business case' for women on boards, often by making claims that adding women to boards will see a financial or reputational return for the company. This is most frequently found in research produced by consulting companies (see, for example, Catalyst, 2004; McKinsey, 2007, 2008, 2010; and Struber, 2012) but is problematic due to it being 'plagued with endogeneity'—an overreliance on correlation rather than causation (Adams, 2016). We do not expand on the business case here in detail, but it is valuable to note that, in spite of its methodological issues, policymakers have drawn heavily on the business benefits of appointing women directors to justify policymaking and far less commonly on a social justice case (see, for example, Davies, 2011; European Commission, 2014).

Research into the characteristics and experiences of women directors—and their similarities or differences to men—has largely been conducted in order to provide explanations for the lack of women on boards. Such research falls broadly into two camps: one, those that look at the human capital aspects of the role, the kinds of experience and traits required for the role and how this may lead to bias towards men. The second takes a social capital perspective, noting the reliance on networks for recruitment and arguing that women are excluded due to their networks being insufficient to gain them access to those recruiting for board roles. While there are limitations across this field (see Kirsch, 2018), we raise here an epistemological problem. As we will demonstrate, these perspectives have relied on a functionalist and positivist 'body counting' starting point (Calás *et al.*, 2014; Martin, 2001) that treats gender solely as a category for comparison rather than as something continuously 'done' (West and Zimmerman, 1987) or 'performed' (Butler, 1990). The majority of the field of women on boards research draws on essentialist notions of gender. Some recent work shows how gender theories can be fruitfully used in research on gender on boards. Clarke's (2019) Foucauldian analysis of websites and annual reports of 30 FTSE 100 companies shows how women are represented either as saviours, with their essentialist skills and talents viewed as necessary for organisational success, or subordinates, where essentialist characteristics are viewed as deficient and requiring assistance. However, such research is the exception rather than the rule in the field, and most research aligns with either human and/or social capital perspectives.

The Human Capital Argument

Research into women on boards has often looked at the career backgrounds, experiences and qualifications of women directors in comparison to men's. This typically presumes that there is a human capital (Becker, 1964) or 'individual deficit' explanation (Gutek, 1994) for women's absence: women are not appointed to boards because they lack the necessary experience, qualifications or skills desired for board positions (Burke, 2000; Bushell, 2015; Hillman and Dalziel, 2003; Nicholson and Kiel, 2004; Talmud and Izraeli, 1999). This has been counteracted by a wealth of research that has pointed to women directors' apparent 'over-qualification' for board roles. For instance, research finds that women typically hold higher formal qualifications than men on the same boards and are more likely to have advanced degrees and MBAs, as well as international experience (Burgess and Theranou, 2000, 2002; Menèndez and González, 2012; Peterson and Philpot, 2007; Sheridan, 2001; Sheridan and Milgate, 2005; Sheridan *et al.*, 2015; Singh *et al.*, 2008; Terjesen *et al.*, 2008). Researchers in these studies tend to come to the conclusion then that women are held to higher standards than men for the same roles. This counteracts the idea that in order to get more women on boards, standards are dropped.

Another key and consistent finding is that boards have a preference for people with previous board experience (Ahern and Dittmar, 2012; Davies, 2011; Doldor *et al.*, 2012; Fahlenbrach *et al.*, 2011; Fich and White, 2005; Zorn, 2004). This can be a significant barrier for women, as there are relatively few who have been in these roles. This may be intuitive: as directors are responsible for making strategic decisions for the organisation, they must demonstrate competence by having previously been directors or holding high-level senior business positions (Hill, 1995; Johnson *et al.*, 1996; Sealy and Doherty, 2012; Sheridan *et al.*, 2015). However, there is also evidence to suggest that this is symbolic rather than practical. There is a presumed 'liability of newness' (Kor and Misangyi, 2008) to candidates who do not already have a board role. Previous board experience, therefore, acts as an indicator to the appointing boards that a candidate is not reputationally risky (Fahlenbrach et al., 2011; Gaughan, 2013). This might be particularly important for women: Hawarden and Marsland (2011) found that female and minority directors are typically added to boards faster than white men but only once they have substantive board experience, suggesting that the 'liability of newness' is less of a barrier to white men (Hawarden and Marsland, 2011: p. 536, see also Hawarden, 2010; Hillman *et al.*, 2002). This is often related to the golden skirts phenomenon where it is presumed that in order to meet targets or quotas, a handful of women hold multiple board roles—although it should be noted that this phenomenon is frequently overstated (Seierstad and Opsahl, 2011). Again, this suggests that women are held to both higher and different standards than men for the same roles. It also suggests that once women have received the stamp of approval by one board, they might become attractive to other boards because they are perceived as less risky.

Requirements also vary according to sector and industry, which can also contribute to gendered differences. Partly in response to an increased focus on regulation and risk since the 2008 financial crisis, financial backgrounds and qualifications are increasingly desirable to boards (Lowe *et al.*, 2018; Roberts, 2015; Zorn, 2004). Given the gender imbalance that occurs within financial industries and the relatively few women who make it to very senior roles, a preference for financial backgrounds may disproportionality benefit men. Conversely, Sealy and Doherty (2012) found that of the women appointed to FTSE 100 board positions in 2012, 57% came from a financial background or held financial qualifications. They conclude that finance can be a 'springboard' for women into board positions (Sealy and Doherty, 2012). They also found that candidates described coming from a finance background as a way to tackle address gendered expectations around board roles. Financial qualifications were perceived as levelling the playing field for women to allow them to appear as similar as possible to men and to speak the language of the board (Sealy and Doherty, 2012). Although not identified in their report, these findings suggest that even where there are preferences for certain kinds of experience or background, how candidates mobilise this experience to get roles is subject to gendered biases. Here it is suggested that women—as well as having the right experience—must use that experience to accentuate their similarities with men and overcome assumptions about their 'emotional' nature.

While the human capital explanation is a natural starting point to explaining women's absence from the boardroom, much of the research that either supports or refutes the human capital explanation does not sufficiently explain *how* lacking the right experience results in women being excluded (see, for example, Burke, 2000; Terjesen *et al.*, 2009; Singh *et al.*, 2008; Hillman *et al.*, 2007), and it presupposes that the process is meritocratic, even while arguing that it is biased. Mattis (2000), for example, cites a 1993 Catalyst survey wherein CEOs stated their reluctance to appoint women due to a belief that they are 'unqualified'; Bushell (2015) states that 'CEOs and headhunters frequently cite lack of human capital as a reason for not selecting women board members', referring to research that does not actually study the appointment process. It is suggested that those who select board members regularly assume that women lack human capital and thus the required expertise and knowledge (Gabaldon *et al.* 2016). While women's 'over-qualification' can be demonstrated empirically, it is not clear how this is relevant to the appointment process and perhaps over-relies on a presumption that the board appointment process is rational and meritocratic (Hillman *et al.*, 2000; Hillman and Dalziel, 2003; Johnson *et al.*, 1996).

When we look wider at the corporate governance literature, we also find that there is no clear definition of what experience, skills and competencies are needed for boards (Bushell, 2015), either in the UK or globally (Zattoni and Cuomo, 2010). While financial backgrounds and previous board experience are most common, many directors do not have either. In a review of global corporate governance codes, Zattoni and Cuomo (2010) concluded that there was little consensus as to what skills and experience are needed by directors, and it was generally presumed that boards would recruit a relevant mix of skills, ensuring balance across the board members, while ensuring a fit with the specific needs of the company. This again highlights the importance of understanding wider social discourses and how they influence which directors may be more desired than others rather than the criteria representing a typical job role description that may be seen elsewhere in recruitment.

The Skill Set

The corporate governance literature also suggests that the aspiring director's assessment is—more so than for other kinds of roles—based on highly subjective and personal criteria, as the role is seen to require certain personality types and interpersonal skills. Directors are seen to need excellent communication skills and leadership qualities (Burke, 1997a, 1997b; Tricker and Lee, 1997), intellectual ability, good judgement, high level of integrity, analytical thinking and ability to be constructive, collaborative and diplomatic (Korn/Ferry, 2012). Although many of these traits are to be expected in senior roles, directors' traits are often described as qualitatively different: an emphasis is placed on being inspirational and visionary (Eagly and Karau, 2002; House and McGrath, 2004; McCauley, 2004; Vinkenburg *et al.*, 2011) and on high-level decision making and strategic thinking (Tricker and Lee, 1997). This is felt by directors too: when asked what made them suitable for the role, women directors in Sheridan and Milgate's (2005) research cited their communication skills, leadership qualities and fit with the board (and, crucially, rarely mention their human capital or the over-qualification we discussed earlier). This belief, therefore, legitimates a focus on board members' personal characteristics, traits and social skills (Stern and Westphal, 2010). Westphal and Stern (2007) argue that directors can negotiate this and gain positions through tactics such as flattery, opinion conformity and favour rendering (Westphal and Stern, 2006, 2007; Westphal, 1998) but that these practices are more beneficial for white men than for groups with lower status. A focus on subjective skills may, therefore, disadvantage women.

In much of the literature there is also emphasis placed on directors' independence and ability to influence. The role of the director has traditionally been centred on the protection of shareholder interests; they are there to provide independent control over the management on behalf of shareholders (Fama, 1980; Hillman and Dalziel, 2003; Walt and Ingley, 2003; Westphal and Graebner, 2010; Westphal and Milton, 2000). They must, therefore, also be able to challenge and influence the executive directors and board decision-making (Pye, 2000, 2002; Stevenson and Radin, 2009; Westphal, 1999; Zajac and Westphal, 1996). Westphal and Stern (2007) argue that women and/or ethnic minorities typically have to work harder to achieve this influence in the boardroom due to their perceived lower status than their white, male colleagues. Women are also expected to be less influential when they join a board as they are 'out group' members in men's spaces (Carter *et al.*, 2010; Westphal and Milton, 2000; Zhu *et al.*, 2014).

Wider research into gender and leadership is also relevant here. This has demonstrated that women's leadership styles, voice and presentation of self are all held to different, often higher, standards than men (Wajcman, 1999; Rutherford, 2001). Women may have greater difficulty demonstrating 'executive presence' (Hewlett, 2014), something crucial for gaining senior positions and board roles. This is supported by the wealth of gender and organisations research that points to the intrinsically masculine nature of organisations and how they implicitly exclude women, particularly at senior levels (Acker, 1990, 1992; Kanter, 1977; Cockburn, 1991). Senior positions of power and influence in corporate life are 'masculinised' in that they tend to be constructed around male norms (Mavin *et al.*, 2014). Women in senior or elite roles, therefore, face a 'double-bind' due to their occupying a space where they have to perform the role of the elite leader (who is inherently masculine) while meeting contradictory expectations related to notions of (respectable) femininity (Mavin and Grandy, 2016a, 2016b; Mavin *et al.*, 2014).

A focus on personal presentation also disadvantages women in senior roles. Women leaders typically have to work harder to ensure credibility and respectability via their appearance through adherence to rules that can be ambiguous, complex and contradictory (Kelan, 2013). Their place in leadership is influenced by expectations of what is deemed respectable: 'what should be worn, what mannerisms, demeano[u]r, voice, size and shape are appropriate' (Sinclair, 2011: p. 119). This, Mavin and colleagues argue, means that women need to do gender 'well' (through performing femininity) while also doing gender 'differently' (performing masculinity) (Mavin and Grandy, 2013, 2016a, 2016b; Mavin *et al.*, 2014). While this has been noted in the experiences of women in senior roles, it has not been explicitly adopted in the women-on-boards literature or connected with the specificities of the director role.

On the other hand, there is an opposing wealth of research to suggest that women's leadership styles are increasingly more valued by organisations, being more collaborative, transformational and effective (Eagly and Carli, 2007). Roberts (2015) argues that the global financial crisis in 2008 was a notable pivotal moment for the business case for gender equality because analysis of the crisis often attributed it, in part, to the testosterone-heavy, risk-taking environments that the banks operated in, which women were largely absent from. This allowed for the '(re)emergence of the business case for gender equality' (Roberts, 2015: p. 214). A 'women-as-saviours' narrative surfaced, where women were viewed as key to economic recovery due to stereotypical, gendered assumptions that they are more risk averse than men and a belief that they can moderate the excessively risky and testosterone-driven behaviour of men simply with their presence in organisations or boardrooms (McDowell, 2011; Prügl, 2012).

The Notion of Fit

A third and final strand of research relating to directors' characteristics that is relevant to this research is that which demonstrates that directors are frequently judged by how they 'fit' with the current board (Hill, 1995; Pye, 2000, 2001). A report by the UK's Equality and Human Rights Commission (EHRC) into how directors are appointed concluded that often appointing board members use their 'gut instincts' to judge candidates' potential value, assessing how the individual would fit with the 'values, norms and behaviours of existing board members' (Doldor *et al.*, 2012: p. iv). The authors argue that this reliance on 'fit' inevitably excludes women, as boards are gender-imbalanced environments that women are less likely to fit into[3] (Doldor *et al.*, 2012; see also Pye, 2002; Sealy and Doherty, 2012).

The appointment process for directors is frequently managed or run by a search firm, and this has implications for fit too. Although not specific to the case of non-executive directors, ethnographic research by Wirz (2014) has demonstrated that subjectivity and fit is an 'inexorable element of the search process, regardless of the sophistication or objectivity of measures in place' (Wirz, 2014: p. 8). Headhunters in Wirz's study stated that their role supporting clients in seeking candidates for senior roles is often made difficult when clients state, "I don't know what I am looking for, but I'll know when I find him" [sic] (Wirz, 2014: p. 7); the candidate who is preferred can rely heavily on the pool of candidates' interactions with the CEO or chair. Meriläinen and colleagues (2013) also found evidence for this specifically in relation to a candidate's appearance. They argue that an individual's potential to fill positions is often judged using embodied capability measures, such as physical fitness, voice and appearance. This disadvantages those who do not fit this 'ideal'.

A problem with the criticism of this judgement on 'fit' is that when we turn to the corporate governance literature, we also find that 'fit' may be an explicit requirement for candidates to be seen as good directors (Sheridan *et al.*, 2011). McGregor (2000) argues that board recruitment is less concerned with the traits of individual directors because the board requires a mix of skills to be effective. Similarly, Hill's (1995) research into board behaviour found that directors feel that 'consensus' is an important aspect of board discussions, viewing the boards they sat on as 'unitary bodies, small teams of colleagues working together on a consensual basis, with collective responsibility[4] for the direction of their organization' (Hill, 1995: p. 256). Gaughan (2011), drawing on her research into FTSE 100 boards, found that candidates were regarded as entering the ranks of a corporate elite and, therefore, need to have a cultural fit with the norms and values of its other members to ensure that they do not pose a reputational risk. In terms of addressing gender bias in the process, this is problematic, as it suggests that assessing candidates' 'fit' with the board is not necessarily incongruous with a belief that the process is meritocratic.

The extant research into women on boards presents a number of explanations for why women may be excluded from boards of directors that relate to the individuals seeking board work. There are differences in men and women's levels of business experience, which is presumed to result in a preference for men, as they are more likely to possess senior business experience. A substantial proportion of the women on boards literature has taken this as its starting point (see, for example, Terjesen *et al.*, 2008; Gabaldon *et al.*, 2016), as it provides an important connection to wider research on gender and organisation: the barriers facing women getting to the top of organisations result in relatively few women with senior business experience, meaning there are too few women with the right experience to be chosen for boards. Research also suggests that men may more easily demonstrate the personal traits associated with director roles and be more desired by boards; they may also be more likely to 'fit' with the board. This is supported by our wider understandings of how women are excluded from senior roles through gendered expectations on how they should look, behave and be.

While this can go some way to explaining gender imbalance on boards, there are significant limitations to these explanations. First, the field is limited by a lack of specific, empirical research and relies instead on inference. For human capital explanations, the majority build on publicly available data regarding directors characteristics, and for research on the right personality or fitting in with the board, the emphasis is on applying wider theoretical work rather than conducting primary research into how these factors work in practice. Second, all three explanations exclusively focus on how competence is defined through the process of appointment, concluding that women and men are judged differently. This treats director recruitment as a rational or neutral process, which produces gender imbalance rather than examining the process itself. To sum up, while aiming to account for broader processes and areas of bias in their explanations for women's absence, research uses orientations that start from the aim of comparing men and women directors and largely relying on the accounts of current directors.

The Board Appointment Process

Zooming out from focusing on the individual-level characteristics of board directors, we also need to examine the process by which directors are identified and chosen for roles. Non-executive recruitment is characterised by its opacity and reliance on recommendations, personal networks and reputation (Doldor *et al.*, 2012; EHRC, 2016; Gaughan, 2013). It is also a market dominated by search firms. The corporate governance literature has both acknowledged and criticised the opacity of the director appointment process (see, for instance, Adams *et al.*, 2010; Finkelstein *et al.*, 2009; Johannisson and Huse, 2000; Withers *et al.*, 2012), typically out of concern for the demographics and diversity levels of boards (Doldor *et al.*, 2012). It is also assumed that the selection of directors will affect board effectiveness or director independence

(Adams *et al.*, 2010; Hermalin and Weisbach, 1988), particularly given the focus placed on non-executives being independent to the board.

Historically non-executive directors were chosen by the chair or CEO (Withers *et al.*, 2012); however, in recent years, there have been moves to make the process more rigorous through the increased use of nomination committees and headhunters to identify candidates.[5] The UK Corporate Governance Code (Financial Reporting Council, 2018) states that companies should be transparent in their board appointment processes, either by publicly advertising roles or using executive search firms/headhunters.[6] This is intended to encourage rigour and objectivity in the process and discourage boards from appointing people they already know (Gabaldon *et al.*, 2016). The vast majority of corporate board-level roles are not publicly advertised, however, including all of the FTSE 350, and only two-thirds of the FTSE 350 state using a headhunter (EHRC, 2016; Lowe *et al.*, 2018).

A nomination committee is a sub-committee of the board that is responsible for identifying and nominating candidates for board positions. They are presumed to have a positive effect on board diversity by applying greater scrutiny to the appointment process, ensuring that it is as rigorous and fair as possible (Ruigrok *et al.*, 2006, 2007); opening up the process to a wider range of candidates, reducing the influence of the CEO (Westphal and Stern, 2007) and/or dissuading them or the chairs from handpicking candidates from their own personal networks (Doldor *et al.*, 2012; Eminet and Guedri, 2010; Hoskisson *et al.*, 2009). This committee will be made up of non-executive directors and is typically chaired by the chair of the board. While there is some evidence to suggest that the presence of women on the nominations committee has a positive effect on the level of gender diversity (Kaczmarek *et al.*, 2012), contradictory research found that boards with diverse nomination committees were no more likely to appoint women directors (Ruigrok *et al.*, 2007). Overall, the evidence to support nomination committees lead to more diverse appointments is patchy, and, in practice, the chair still has much influence over the process.

Once a vacancy has been identified, the appointing board will typically start by drawing up a specification for the new director and putting together a shortlist of potential candidates. In large companies, this is often done by working with or delegating to an executive search firm[7] (Arfken *et al.*, 2004; Bushell, 2015; Tienari *et al.*, 2013). The primary role of the search firm is the finding and mapping of potential clients (Doldor *et al.*, 2012, 2016): they have access to wide databases of potential candidates and are seen to offer a more professional, rigorous and meritocratic approach than the appointing board contacting people through its own networks (Khurana, 2002; Tienari *et al.*, 2013; Wirz, 2014). This assumption is not widely examined in the literature, however, save a handful of studies that have identified how bias can still occur in search work (Beaverstock *et al.*, 2015).

It is important to highlight that in much of the literature on women on boards, an increase in rigour and professionalism is presumed to promote the appointment of women by neutralising gender bias in the process. After the Davies' review (Davies, 2011) recommended that search firms should and can support gender-balanced boards, they were also encouraged to 'extend their search processes to look deeper and wider into the female talent pool' (Davies, 2015: p. 16). Through this they became cast as 'accidental activists' (Doldor *et al.*, 2016). This had two key consequences. First, it required search firms to address issues inherent in their practice: they were required to sign up to a code of conduct that stated they would articulate and commit to best practices in relation to search criteria processes around board appointments (ibid.). Second, it directly connected the lack of women on boards to the opaque process of appointments, with the inference that the use of headhunters who signed up to the code of conduct could drive change.

One problem with viewing search firms as a driver for change or as necessarily leading to more rigorous practice is demonstrated in the wider research on search firms, which shows that the process of executive search is highly prone to gendered practices. First, it primarily involves white men as headhunters, clients and candidates (Beaverstock *et al.*, 2015; Meriläinen *et al.*, 2013; Dreher *et al.*, 2011; Faulconbridge *et al.*, 2009) and it enforces homogeneity through targeting narrow pools of potential candidates (Khurana, 2002). Second, while the databases of potential candidates[8] that headhunters maintain may make the process more 'open' (a database is likely to be broader than a boards' networks, for instance), they are still created, maintained and updated by the headhunters who have to make (often highly subjective) judgements regarding candidates' competence. This assessment of competence is affected by gender biases similar to those discussed earlier: they rely on specific and narrow kinds of experience, personality traits that may be more easily demonstrated by men and fit with the board (Faulconbridge *et al.*, 2009; Beaverstock *et al.*, 2015; Wirz, 2014).

Third, headhunters also tend to rely on their own networks to source candidates. It has been suggested that headhunters maintain and reproduce hierarchical, restrictive network practices (Faulconbridge *et al.*, 2009). They argue that while they are different than 'Old Boys' networks or the 'gentlemanly capitalism' (Augar, 2008) of the City of London, these networks comprise a new, global elite that dominates in labour markets. While these networks may include women and those from international or global backgrounds, they still hold many of the class and social status markers of the previous Old Boys' networks (cf. Savage and Williams, 2008; Savage *et al.*, 2013; Savage, 2015).

We also have to remember that search firms are a service industry that reflects the needs and requests of its clients. In ethnographic research on search firms, Wirz (2014) found many occasions where women were being put forward for roles to satisfy a gender target set by the client, while the headhunter was aware that the candidates would be rejected because their 'calibre' was not what the client had asked for.[9] Dreher and colleagues (2011) found that white men were more likely than women to be contacted by executive search firms, and this was also highlighted by research we conducted for this project: through a survey of aspirant non-executive directors, we found that women were less likely to have been contacted by search firms, and when they did have contact with them, were more likely to be offered advice rather than roles (Brown *et al.*, 2015). Generally, there is patchy empirical evidence that using search firms makes the appointment process more rigorous or biased in itself or that this will necessarily lead to the appointment of more women (Doldor *et al.*, 2012, 2016).

While much research into the director appointment process highlights its opacity and lack of rigour, this is often stated in relation to what is unknown rather than what is known. Evidence of increasing rigour in the process is presumed but not strictly demonstrated: qualitative research found that chairs of FTSE 100 boards in the UK generally *feel* that the appointment process is becoming more rigorous and objective and moving towards a greater focus on skills, competencies and experience (Doldor *et al.*, 2012; Vinnicombe *et al.*, 2010), and it is assumed that this will lead to more diverse appointments (Vinnicombe *et al.*, 2010). There is a presumed (but empirically unproven) relationship between rigorous appointments and board diversity. Finally, there is an argument made that opaque appointments are necessary. In research into the appointment of FTSE 100 board directors, Gaughan (2013) found that candidates often justified the need for an opaque and lengthy appointment process to protect the reputations of the chair and the company. She argues that as information about director appointments is highly sensitive, non-executive directors (NEDs) and chairs are prepared to engage in processes that are opaque and ambiguous and 'lacking both transparency and formality' (Gaughan, 2013: p. 194).

Visibility and Networking

As the review of the earlier appointment process highlights, how directors are appointed rests significantly on the likelihood of individuals coming into contact with 'gatekeepers' (van den Brink and Benschop, 2014): the chair of the board (Burke, 1997b, 2000; Mattis, 1993, 2000; Sheridan and Milgate, 2005), current board members (particularly those on nomination committees) or executive search firms (Bushell, 2015; Arfken *et al.*, 2004). Candidates' success, therefore, depends on their ability to forge and maintain personal networks of connections with potential appointing boards (Ibarra and Hunter, 2007), and social capital and social network theories are frequently put forward as possible explanations for the lack of women on boards (Bushell, 2015; Gaughan, 2013; Terjesen *et al.*, 2009), as candidates come through networks, and the primary mode of recruitment is appointers reaching out (Elliott, 2000; McDonald, 2010; McDonald and Elder, 2006). This requires the individual to have a 'quality' network (Bushell, 2015), featuring both weak and strong ties[10] (Granovetter, 1973, 1983) to people in positions of power.

Research in this area largely draws on the wider literature into networks where differing networks have been presented as a key explanation for women's difficulty reaching senior positions, particularly in areas where visibility and knowing the right people are prerequisites for success (Ibarra, 1992, 1997; Burgess and Tharenou, 2002). Historically, this research focused solely on the differences between men's and women's networks in terms of structure, usage and outcomes (Ibarra, 1992, 1993, 1995, 1997). This literature has argued that women's networks tend to be narrower, less diverse and contain lower status members (Brass *et al.*, 2004; Ibarra, 1992; Ibarra *et al.*, 2005), and this is often self-reproducing, as individuals are more inclined to network with high-status individuals and with people similar to themselves (Holgersson, 2013). Other research has suggested that even when men and women are of similar seniority and status, women receive fewer benefits from their networks (Ibarra *et al.*, 2010; McGuire, 2000). Women are also excluded from men's informal networking practices and gatherings (Martin, 2003) by gendered expectations and at times literal barriers, such as the continued existence of Old Boys' clubs and all-men private members' clubs.

The way that men and women use their networks is also gendered and moderated by gendered expectations. It has been argued that women are more likely than men to use their networks for support and friendship, while men's networks are more instrumental and can be more easily and readily used for self-promotion, passing information and increasing their own visibility (Forret and Dougherty, 2001; Ibarra, 1992, 1993). Drawing on research with women in senior roles, Mavin and co-authors (2014) offer a more critical feminist perspective, arguing that women's affective connection with their friends prevents them from using workplace friends in an instrumental way because they typically focus on the 'work at hand' and see workplace relationships and friendships as irrelevant to progression. They argue that this is in part to avoid gendered stereotypes, as making friends at work is to fall into a 'feminine' stereotype, and they face judgement from peers or employers, and in part because women's utilisation of workplace friendships goes against meritocratic ideals of how their careers might be furthered. Benschop (2009) similarly found that men and women are constrained by a micro-politics of gendering in their networking practices where women have to emphasise

their professional identity and move away from 'unproductive and feminine sociability' (Benschop, 2009: p. 233), for instance, by emphasising
the instrumental function of their work networks. In contrast, men's professionalism is rarely challenged by their having workplace friendships.

Whilst work on gender differences in networks is helpful in understanding why women's networks may affect their access to boards, gender and organisations scholars have criticised its scope for its treatment
of gender as a salient category and of networks as static, as well as the
utilisation of social capital and networking theories and quantitative
data, all of which neglect (women's) affective accounts (Ibarra, 1992,
1997; Benschop, 2009; Ely and Padavic, 2007). This is to the detriment
of understanding the process and practice of networking. Van den Brink
and Benschop (2014) therefore advocate the adoption of a 'networking
practices' approach, which focuses on what people are 'doing and saying'
in interactions. This, they argue, means examining 'the dynamic, socio-
political actions of building, maintaining, and using relations at work
for personal, career, and organizational benefits (. . .) [such as] maintaining contacts, socializing, forming coalitions, negotiating, and sharing or
withholding information' (van den Brink and Benschop, 2014: p. 463).
By examining how individuals go about building and maintaining their
networks through understanding how their interactions with others contribute to this, research can move beyond a static approach to networks.

Such an approach is highly applicable to understanding gender on the
route to the boardroom, as while much of the research presumes that
visibility and the network are crucial to success, it focuses less on how
these networks are accessed and mobilised, as well as how networking
is done. In both research and policy, there is an underlying assumption
that women simply need to be known by the people making the decisions rather than actively pushing themselves forward (see, for example,
Doldor *et al.*, 2012; McGregor, 2000). Adams and Flynn (2005) conclude that women need to blip as available and competent board candidates on the radar screen. Similarly, Burgess and Tharenou (2000) argue
that an individuals' investment in his or her own experience and skills has
to become visible to allow this individual to be appointed onto a board.
This then treats visibility as a binary trait: either the candidates are visible or not—and this does not account for the multitude of influences on
how individuals' enter and navigate within their networks or how the
way that they network might affect their chances of being visible or of
being appointed.

This is also vital when we consider the reliance on recommendations.
When recruitment is facilitated by gatekeepers—candidates are typically
invited to apply or explicitly directed to a vacancy rather than applying
directly—self-nomination is not welcome from those appointing (van den
Brink and Benschop, 2014). The individual instead has to gain visibility
to gatekeepers or 'scouts' (ibid.) who put them forward. Although van

den Brink and Benschop (2014) do not expand on it in their analysis, this may suggest that individuals who are 'too' targeted with their networking will be less likely to be successful by not following the norms of elite recruitment. This is also supported by research into search firms which has highlighted that headhunters place high significance on their ability to find candidates for their databases and for roles and rarely take individuals who contact them directly or who are not recommended to them by a third party (Faulconbridge *et al.*, 2009; Wirz, 2014).

Mavin and co-authors (2014) argue that the focus on social network analysis has been at the detriment of research into women's affective relationships and friendships in workplace contexts and leaving intra-gender relations (here relations between women) under-researched and under-theorised. This is particularly important given the emergence of an increased presence of women in senior elite roles, problematising the assumption that women's progression is solely a result of their having different networks and/or more heterophilous networks to men.

The tendency to ignore the study of women's workplace relations with other women is also at odds with other areas of the workplace and organisation literature, which commonly contain elements of female solidarity as a recommendation for women's advancement in employment (Mavin *et al.*, 2014). In order to subvert male dominance in the workplace, it is suggested that women need to move beyond token status, form coalitions, become allies, develop support networks and, in doing so, be able to effect cultural change of masculine organisations (Kanter, 1977); this is also seen in the importance placed on women having female mentors and sponsors (Ibarra, 2001; Ibarra *et al.*, 2010), the recommendation of female networks (Bierema, 2005) and a general rhetoric of positivity around women's relationships with other women at work. Mavin and colleagues (2014) have argued that women's ability to have 'positive intra-gender relations' (Mavin, 2006, 2008), forming homophilous, strong friendships or relationships with other women in the workplace, is perceived as offering the potential to enable them to compete and cooperate simultaneously, as men already do to great success. This is also seen in more recent discourses around neoliberal feminism, where connections with other women are frequently presented as a strategic contribution to individual success in the workplace (see, for example, Sandberg, 2013).

One way that organisations, non-governmental organisations and policymakers have gone about seeking to address the lack of women on boards has been through the formation of women-on-boards networks with the aim of increasing women's visibility and strengthening their networks. The assumptions behind this is often that women's networks offer women support and solidarity and opportunities to network in a more formal setting, allowing them to share information and learning experiences with other women (Cross and Armstrong, 2008; O'Neil *et al.*, 2011), with the presumption that this will help women to be successful

(Bierema, 2005; Scott, 1998). This is not always the case: Bierema (2005) found that while women's networks offered a structure that was useful for sharing and in-group support, women felt uncomfortable being a part of it; worrying that they would be perceived as 'male-bashing', 'needing help' or that the network was purely for social reasons. This leads to the conclusion that the emulation of male power structures is not necessarily the best way to improving women's presence in positions of power because of how they are perceived by organisations (Bierema, 2005; O'Neil *et al.*, 2011).

Conclusion

In this chapter, we outlined key aspects that are regularly raised in relation to the board appointment process, which included human capital requirements, the skills needed to be on boards, the notion of fit and the importance of gaining visibility through networking. We thus illuminated how research tries to understand which factors shape women's appointments to boards (Kirsch, 2018). While a lot is known about the structural characteristics and outcomes of networks, the literature as it stands demonstrates that much less is known about the processes of networking and how gender is constructed as part of networking, understanding both gender and networking as dynamic and complex. Through understanding networking as 'practice' and taking a broader account of how networking practices may be gendered (van den Brink and Benschop, 2012; Benschop, 2009), we can show gendered differences in their formation and maintenance. There is a growing literature considering how socio-cultural contexts can constrain and shape network(ing) inequalities (Ely and Padavic, 2007), recognising that networks are not static connections between people and not simply the result of choice or circumstance; rather, they are social constructions (Faulconbridge *et al.*, 2009), influenced by gendered expectations. In the case of women on boards, there is a need to build on the social capital explanation for their absence by examining their networking practices and how they are gendered rather than presuming that their networks are different. There is also a need to understand how they make sense of their relationships with men as gatekeepers but also to understand how they negotiate the increased proportion of women in these spaces: through discourses of competition and/or solidarity. In this chapter, we, therefore, suggest that the literature to date has not paid sufficient attention the sense-making processes of aspiring board members on their journey to the boardroom. Such a perspective can broaden our understanding of gender and boards.

Notes

1. In the US, such individuals are frequently referred to as independent directors, while in the UK, the preferred term is non-executive directors, although

the roles are fairly interchangeable and the literature can be drawn on to apply to both contexts.

2. Morgan Stanley Capital International All-Country World index (MSCI ACWI) companies.

3. It should be noted that although research demonstrates assessment by fit with the board, these studies often take the difference between men and women as a given, presuming that because judgment is on fit and boards are majority men, women will find it difficult to fit in or demonstrate fit.

4. In legal terms, boards are all collectively responsible for the company, and the non-executives are as responsible as the executives in legal terms.

5. Once the director has been identified and chosen, they are 'formally' nominated and put forward to be voted upon by the shareholders (Johnson *et al.*, 1996; Monks and Minow, 2004); while hypothetically they could then be voted against, only one candidate is put forward, and it is very rare for them to not be selected at this stage (Hillman *et al.*, 2011). For this reason, often the appointment process is synonymous with gaining visibility with the appointing board and being selected by the chair or nominations committee. As pointed out by Withers *et al.* (2012), this means that the identification, screening and selection processes are the most significant for understanding how directors are appointed and why these processes may exclude women.

6. In general, 'executive search firm' refers to the organisation, while 'headhunters' refers to the individuals who work in an executive search firm; however, the terms are largely interchangeable in the literature (c.f. Faulconbridge *et al.*, 2009).

7. Due to the confidentiality surrounding the headhunting industry, it is difficult to get an accurate picture of their usage (Faulconbridge *et al.*, 2009) but in 2011, 73% of FTSE 100 companies and 60% of FTSE 250 companies reported using search firms for their board appointments (Sealy *et al.*, 2011); while in 2018, it was 48% of FTSE 350 companies (Lowe *et al.*, 2018).

8. The database is also interesting in terms of maintaining search firms' place in the labour market. While historically it would be understandably impossible for a board to gain quick access to a list of potential candidates for a role, making the role of the search firm more significant, changes such as the Internet, increased use of LinkedIn and the sheer speed with which individuals can be introduced to each other through email could, hypothetically, be presumed to allow for a democratization of the process and for boards to (much more rigorously) conduct their own searches. To address this, search firms have discursively cast the Internet as a potential source of 'information overload' that makes board recruitment more difficult (Faulconbridge et al., 2009; Beaverstock *et al.*, 2015). Search firms, therefore, have to draw on discourses that present their work as 'painstaking' or as needing a great deal of time and skill.

9. If a shortlist has only one minority woman, then this woman has statistically no chance of being selected (Johnson *et al.*, 2016).

10. Weak ties provide the individual with 'non-redundant' connections to other individuals; whilst those individuals may not be guarantees of assistance, a wide spread of connections will mean the individual has access to a great deal of information. In the context of board appointments, this will affect which board positions the candidate knows about. The strength of strong ties comes in the obligation to reciprocation that the tie implies; weak ties are more likely to have access to information, but those with strong ties are more likely to offer that information up (Granovetter, 1973, 1983).

3   The Ideal Board Member

Research on the ideal worker has a long tradition in studies on gender, work and organisation that builds on Acker's (1990) seminal article. This body of work shows how the idea of an ideal worker permeates current workplaces by privileging those who conform to type and making them more likely to be recruited and promoted. Often, those ideas around the ideal worker are implicit, unspoken and unconscious; candidates for recruitment and promotion just 'feel right' or 'fit in'. In this chapter, we outline how this concept applies to board work and how the idea of an 'ideal' board member is constructed. The ideal is someone who has the 'right' experience personality traits and who 'fits with the board'. Aspiring directors described themselves in relation to this ideal, using it to explain how the board appointment process works and accounts for their motivation to seek roles, as well as their success or difficulty in getting roles. First, we show how having the 'right experience' relates to candidates' motivations for seeking director roles. Their narratives place high importance on specific kinds of high-profile experience, and they describe their career backgrounds to fit with what boards are presumed to value. This will show how certain kinds of experience—in particular previous board experience—are seen as highly prized and useful when seeking board roles. It will also show how this perception of the ideal experience is reflected in what is deemed the 'wrong' experience and how those individuals with the 'wrong' experience describe how they are discursively 'othered' through being described as 'wild-card' candidates. It will also explore the personal characteristics and personality traits that they see as important for becoming a good director and how these are gendered, subjective and individualistic. Finally, we show how the concept of 'fit' emerges in candidates' accounts. The emphasis on 'fit' allows the interpretation of the 'ideal' board member to be highly subjective while simultaneously rationalising and defending the board recruitment process and discursively rendering it objective.

The 'Right' Experience

When describing their reasons for wanting to become a director, our interviewees frequently referred to their suitability for board roles through listing their major career achievements, outlining how they have the right experience and career background for the role. Sarah's[1] account is typical of this kind of introduction.

SARAH [FIRST INTERVIEW]: So my working background and personal background; so, I am a 45-year-old woman. I have three young children under 5. I am not married, and I have worked for most of my career in [Large tech company 1] (.) For much of the time that I worked there, I ran the international online businesses, so my primary role was either as a marketing director or as a general manager. [It was] expanding internationally (.) in some instances starting up businesses like the one we did in China. Then when I left there as (.) Well, a couple of points I suppose about that so in terms of seniority I got quite senior in the organisation. I became a partner. I won the Chairman's Award for business transformation. [Company CEO] only gives out seven a year, so they are fairly exclusive and highly sought after. Then I left there in 2008 to have my first child and whilst on maternity leave, [Company 1] re-organised, and I was headhunted to join [Company 2] as the chief marketing officer, globally. I stayed there for a further two years. I sat on both the [Company 2] UK board, sat on all the boards of the businesses in all of the countries I was responsible for, so six different boards. I chaired two of those as well, and I sat on the main board of the subsidiary boards. So I have got a very strong commercial background. Up until the point I worked for [Company 2] I'd pretty much always had revenue control and P&L [profit and loss] control. I am used to running organisations of up to 500 plus individuals, controlling budgets of half-a-billion US dollars.

To start, it is notable how Sarah describes her career narrative in such a way to demonstrate her ability to be a good director. She refers to a range of indicators or markers of her seniority and significance, and the language she uses to describe it sees her taking ownership over her success ('I ran'; 'I became a partner'; 'I won the (. . .) award') and marks her as senior and extraordinary, emphasising the exclusivity of the award, for example. She also highlights her high level of responsibility: experience in senior business roles, revenue, P&L and budget control and the number of employees all act as indicators of her high-profile qualification for board work, and she emphasises how she was recognised for her ability in these roles. Overall, her narrative presents her as a highly successful business leader with a strong career background in board-relevant areas. This was typical of interviewees' accounts and is in line with wider research, which emphasises the human capital required by candidates seeking board roles.

Discussion of childcare and caring responsibilities was not common in the research, in in large part because the average age of non-executives and our interviewees is 50+ and, therefore, above typical child-rearing age. However, it is worth noting how Sarah incorporates discussion of her children. She starts her career narrative by declaring her children and that she is unmarried, perhaps with the implication that they had affected her career or were a significant part of her identity or career story. They are then interwoven in the narrative: visible but also compartmentalised. She discusses her maternity leave with the company's re-organisation and her being headhunted, downplaying the influence of her children or domestic situation in favour of business-led explanations. At the same time, this could also suggest a kind of 'having it all' discourse: presenting herself as highly successful (perhaps even more successful) by emphasising that she has achieved a senior career and had children while being unmarried. Looking at it that way, her domestic responsibilities are adopted to emphasise her ability while still maintaining a business focus to the narrative.

Although they came from a range of career backgrounds and their experiences were diverse, candidates also often used similar discursive repertoires to describe their careers and thus their suitability for board work. The aspects of their experience mentioned frequently reflected those found in the literature and discussed in the review of the extant literature: they emphasised their high-level business experience, leadership responsibilities and senior or director roles.

GARY [FIRST INTERVIEW]: I'm from [place], I went to [name] school, the local grammar school there, and then I went to Cambridge to read modern languages. I joined [FTSE 100 bank] on their graduate programme. That was where I met Linda[2] actually; she was there. So I then had a career in banking. Sort of all of my career in banking. The last half of my career was at [global bank] where I worked in a whole range of different things. I lived in Hong Kong, but I ran our North-East Asian business, which is, Hong Kong is our biggest business, and then essentially expanded our business into China. Then I came back to the UK, and I ran our Africa business. I was here for Africa; we have a very big business in Sub-Saharan Africa. I became what we call the CIO, chief information officer, which is the head of Technology and Operations. And I headed Strategy, went on the board of the bank, head of Risk and what we call the west side. I was the governance head of Middle East, Africa, Europe and America. So we divided the world in two, someone had Asia, and I had the rest. So that's how it was really. I retired from there in 2010 and became— for a number of personal and career reasons, all very positive by the way, and I thought I'd pursue a more balanced 'plural career' as I call it. Non-executive. I had already become a non-executive director in 2005 of [company], which is a [place]-based London Stock Exchange–listed engineering company (.) They're international and very successful, actually.

Like Sarah, Gary's career narrative emphasises his seniority of specific industry experience: his career in banking, specialist industry background, global and international experience and previous experience of governance and being in the boardroom. He also focuses on the roles that were C-suite (i.e. being CIO) and director level and in doing so implies that these were valuable for moving into director roles; his motivation for seeking board roles is the fact that he has already held board roles.

Methodological literature on life history suggests that often interviewees present messy and inaccurate accounts of their lives, advising the researcher (and audience) not to expect that they will be neat or chronological (McDowell, 1998). In contrast, our respondents told neat, chronological narratives regarding their career histories (cf. McDowell, 1998), suggesting that they are well rehearsed. This could be seen as part of their self-promotion and impression management, where they use aspects of their career history to present themselves in the strongest light. The neatness also suggests these are repeated and practised narratives.

The emphasis placed on having the right experience (particularly board-level experience) was particularly evident in the accounts of those who held the most senior roles. Stephen, for instance, provided a very short answer to the opening question of the interview and focused solely on being a finance director for a FTSE 100 company.

STEPHEN [FIRST INTERVIEW]: Okay, so forget all the early bits, but I've been on the board of [FTSE 100 company] as finance director since, well, finance director designate since the middle of 2005 and officially finance director since the first of January 2006. ^so, I've been on the board eight years or so^ and about = in about 2011, I decided I'd like to take on a non-exec role.

As we also saw in Sarah and Gary's accounts, Stephen refers to his director experience, emphasising that he is a finance director for a FTSE 100 (and by inference) that nothing about his career before then has any relevance to his suitability for boards. This reflects a general assumption in the literature (see, for example, Sealy and Doherty, 2012)—that those with senior finance experience are in high demand for board roles. His response is also direct and shorter than, for example, Sarah, whose description is more focused on pointing to how her broad experience fits into a board. It could also be argued that Stephen's account is a way of emphasising his elite status through his modes of interaction and the way he describes it: the fact that he is a finance director is deemed enough of an explanation. This results in him guiding the interview, stating that he is not going to discuss his career history by saying 'forget the early bits', thus dismissing his early experiences as unimportant and irrelevant.

In subsequent interviews, Stephen referred back to his role frequently and alludes to its significance in leading to his success.

STEPHEN [SECOND INTERVIEW]: But you know, there aren't that many FTSE 100 finance directors who want to do non-exec audit committee chair roles (. . .) So I was kind of unique-ish, well unique, but in a select group, so that skill set is in demand.

Stephen's mention of his current role is again presented here in such a way to highlight his rarity and indicates or reiterates a belief that he will be (or has been) successful because he is the ideal candidate.

SCARLETT [THIRD INTERVIEW]: So did you get any helpful feedback from the headhunters at that stage?
STEPHEN: Not really. They all said, you've just the right credentials for the chairman of audit committee, that you should, you know, find this (.) you'll find the right thing, just give it time.
SCARLETT: And what was it about your credentials that they said was perfect?
STEPHEN: Well-qualified (.) chartered accountant, finance director, multinational company, executive, good reputation, no baggage (. . .). And no skeletons.

In his third interview, Stephen again asserts that he has the 'right experience', relating it this time in relation to headhunters' comments. When asked what that entails, he listed his high-profile experience: referring to the finance experience, previous director role, international experience and executive status; the ideal director has this background. He also mentions reputational aspects by asserting that he has a good reputation and no 'baggage' or 'skeletons'—presumably a reference to having 'skeletons in the closet', which would represent potential reputational risk. Both the visibility of directors and the importance of having a good reputation are common in corporate elites (Gaughan, 2013), particularly for directors of publicly limited companies that are largely in the public eye and encouraged by the UK Corporate Governance Code to report on their directors' backgrounds (FRC, 2018). Taking the three interviews together highlights the durability of the 'right experience' discourse and how it can be used across different occasions for slightly different discursive ends but in all cases to emphasise that s/he is a high-calibre candidate with the right experience who will, at some stage, be successful.

The way that headhunters are described and discursively utilised also suggests that they have a role in dictating and reproducing what constitutes the 'right experience'.

LINDA [FIRST INTERVIEW]: The feedback I've had from the search agents is, "Well, you know, your profile is very much in demand".

For those who felt they had the right experience, feedback from head-hunters was a common way of asserting that in the research interviews: as in the quote from Linda, they often stated that the headhunters described their experience or 'profile' as highly desirable for boards. Similarly, in the earlier extract, Stephen mobilises the headhunters' feedback in the interview to assert that he has the right experience. This results in a kind of reproductive or cyclical truth effect where headhunters' preference for certain kinds of candidates is used as an interpretive repertoire in the research interviews, and this perpetuates the idea that boards are only looking for certain kinds of candidates. By presenting their statements as evidence for their suitability for roles, the interviewees casts themselves as ideal candidates and give power to the headhunter to dictate the ideal (see also Faulconbridge *et al.*, 2009).

In a subsequent interview, Linda again draws on the right experience discourse to make sense of her success; she had, since the last interview, been 'bombarded' (her word) with offers for boards.

SCARLETT: And what do you think it is about your experience or your personality—or your quick wit that makes them?

LINDA [SECOND INTERVIEW]: I don't think it's any of that. I think I'm in a sweet spot at this point. I could probably be green and have a head like a cabbage, and they'd still take me. They're after people with [risk experience] in financial services, because under CRD4 [Capital Requirements Directive] the majority of banks are being required to have a risk committee; they need people with risk experience. (.) If they can fill a quota for Mervyn Davies at the same time and have somebody presentable, then you're halfway there. So for me, being a risk person and female.

SCARLETT: And there's not a lot of you about?

LINDA: There's not a lot of men about! (.) so that helps. I'm under no illusions.

Linda refers again to having the right experience and specifically relates it to recent legislative changes and an increased need for candidates with risk and financial experience. It is notable, therefore, that here Linda draws on these discourses to assert her rarity and states that she is so unusual in her background that she is in a 'sweet spot' and will, by infer-ence, expect to find it easy to get roles. Again, the power of being the ideal candidate makes it seem as though the process will be easy for them.

This idea of themselves as rare and unusual aligns with other accounts we heard where candidates emphasise both the seniority and specific-ity of their experience and locate themselves in an elite position. This impression management has been found in other interview research with board directors (Westphal, 2010) and upholds the rare, elite and exclusive nature of corporate board roles while still maintaining an impression of the process as highly rational and led primarily by market forces.

The Best Way to Become a NED? Be One Already

One specific kind of experience often discussed by candidates as being highly desired by boards was to already or previously have been on a board.

DANIEL [SECOND INTERVIEW]: I forget who it was; it was a chap at [company name], the headhunters, they do a lot of FTSE non-exec work, very strong board practices, and he said, "The best way of getting a non-exec position is to already have a non-exec position". And it is kind of self-perpetuating: once people know you've been through the mill successfully and served out [a] full term with another company and it's a serious company, then you kind of pass muster. People who try to break into that world for the first time I think face a real problem.

The idea that 'the best way of getting a non-exec position is to already have a non-exec position' was a strong discourse through the research; all interviewees drew on this discourse at some point, either in relation to their views on the ideal board member or (as discussed in subsequent chapters) to account for their success or failure (Brown *et al.*, 2015).

MATTHEW [SECOND INTERVIEW]: And then I talked to a bunch of head-hunters, just sent my CV to people who were working in the NED space and they mostly were receptive, met with me, said they would be happy to put me up for things but actually very few have done anything.
SCARLETT: Why do you think that is?
MATTHEW: My experience is that once you have a couple [of director roles], and you are an easy shoo-in, they're desperate to talk to you. If they think they'll get repeat business from you, they're desperate to put you up and talk to you, but if you're new to the game, they won't include you unless they can't get any other names.

Here Matthew refers to the importance of already being a director for getting board roles, in this case attributing it to headhunters' preference for directors with experience and accounting for why he has not yet been put forward for roles. He discusses what others felt was a 'catch 22' situation, where in order to be considered for NED roles they had to already have one, and getting their first was the biggest challenge. For Matthew, this is specifically related to headhunters' practice: a candidate with board experience is an 'easy shoo-in', which presumably means that the candidate will find it very easy to be successful, and therefore head-hunters are not interested in those who do not have this experience.

Although this was more widely discussed in relation to non-executive director experience, there were also some who felt that not having held a C-suite or director role meant they would not be considered for non-executive roles.

MATTHEW [SECOND INTERVIEW]: I do think it is still the case that hiring a front-office-type person seems to be a natural knee-jerk choice for NEDs: 'If you have run a business, you are going to know how to help our board', and I think that by definition my market is much smaller. I'm looking for a board that wants diversity of my type. Whereas if you are an ex-CEO [chief executive officer], an under-writer or a CFO [chief financial officer], those constraints don't apply because the perception will always be [that] you know how companies run, you know what the issues are, we haven't got to fit you in some special box; all opportunities are open. So, I don't know, if there's 200 vacancies a year of NEDs, that first group are always going to see all of them. By definition, I am only going to see the ones that have already [turned down]—so the good news is there may not be as many people like me looking, so that might help, but I don't think it is enough. And I think it will always be biased. [If they] have got a really good CFO, CEO, or a back-office guy? They're going to go with them, and I can't fix that.

In Matthew's account, we see how significant he feels that having held a 'C-suite' role is through his assertion that if he was to have this then 'all opportunities are open'. It is notable that Matthew describes this as a kind of 'bias' towards those individuals who have the right experience, and one that he cannot change. This highlights the strength of the right experience discourse; where it is seen to trump all other factors draws on a discourse where having the right experience is prioritised, obfuscating or downplaying all other factors.

In a similar way to Daniel, Martin's account is critical of the process; however, his reference to boards' preference for previous board experi-ence as a 'natural' or 'knee-jerk' reaction suggests it is an implicit part of the process and necessarily cannot be changed, challenged or negotiated. Even as they criticise the system for being 'biased' or presenting a 'real problem' for new NEDs, there is little discursive space for criticising the premise that if he had the right experience, he would be successful. The emphasis on having the right experience is, therefore, maintained.

CHARLOTTE [SECOND INTERVIEW]: What I've been told by a number of the headhunters and the recruiters in this space, and, in fact, also some of the chairmen on the FTSE 100 that I've been spending a bit of time with is, "You would do so much better to go back into a corporate world, go and do a CFO of a listed entity and you [will] then be jumping out of a tenth floor into a non-exec rather than jumping out of a sixth floor and trying to find a non-exec". And there's something about that, but there's also something for me about: do I really want to go and just do time in a CFO role?

Here again we see the role that headhunters and, in this case, chairmen (sic) play in influencing candidates' perceptions of the ideal board member and how they interpret the process. Having the right experience is given such priority that Charlotte is told (and here reproduces the idea) that it would be easier for her to get a non-executive board role if she was to go into a CFO role and that this would lead to her 'jumping out of a tenth floor': being of higher status and having higher status experience, which she could leverage to get a non-exec role. This is discussed so instrumentally and 'matter-of-factly' that there is little discussion in her statement of specific aspects of that experience she 'needs' to be a good director: it is described as 'doing time' rather than learning specific skills or (as is particularly interesting, given the reliance on networking discussed in the subsequent chapter) building her network.

CHARLOTTE [THIRD INTERVIEW]: So, you know the progress of the non-exec stuff has probably continued as before which is lots of sort of conversations, shortlistings. But the clear message coming back from a number of the chairmen is, "Look if you go and do a CFO role, just do it, and do it as the person who's standing up to do the results announcement and leading it in a FTSE world. It will be a tick-box exercise that goes you know what? You absolutely can be the chair of the audit risk committee, and you absolutely can sit on a listed entities board". (.) And you know, I suppose I faltered for long enough, and I just went well, "okay, it's a game and in some ways, I sort of need to play that".

In the later interview, Charlotte's account is remarkably similar to what she described in her earlier interview, again stating a belief (reiterated by high-profile people she is in contact with) that if she goes into a CFO role, she will then find it much easier to get a board role. This shows why this is presumed to make a difference to her chances: by taking this role, she will be gaining visibility in the 'FTSE world' as someone credible with the right experience, but she also describes it as a tick-box exercise. This draws on a similar matter of fact and highly matter-of-fact attitudes of having the right experience, where experience is viewed as something inflexible and candidates 'just' have to have it to be considered. Although we do not discuss it in detail in this book, this focus on senior-level experience also has the knock-on effect of limiting the 'ideal' board member to someone who is of a particular age. Charlotte was one of the younger interviewees (circa 40), and the average age of a non-executive director in the FTSE 350 was 63 at the time of writing.

The 'Wrong' Experience

As well as accounts that give a clear position on what the right experience is for non-executive roles, interviewees frequently described themselves as having the wrong experience and the challenges they face in being successful.

Peter was retiring from a role as a senior partner in a Big Four accountancy firm. Those who had worked in partnership organisations (such as accountancies or legal firms) often discussed the difficulty they faced in translating their experience into non-executive board roles.

PETER [SECOND INTERVIEW]: So I embarked on this, actually probably wrongly, believing that I would have (.) sort of a passport? From having built a business which, when I started as the senior, effectively being CEO or executive chair, it had a turnover of £150 million. So I thought that was quite a good springboard. So I was sort of quite NAIVELY surprised to find that the listed company board is quite a narrow club. = I hadn't anticipated that people would sort of welcome you with open arms, but I did think they would be able to make the connection between one business which made £150 million a year and another! HEHE. And the message you continually get is that you don't have the (.) the RIGHT sort of experience, or you don't—well you don't really get a clear message, actually.

Here Peter describes his experience being 'wrong'—i.e. he has experience that should be valuable to boards, but boards do not see the value. His use of words such as 'passport' and 'springboard' that imply easy entering or guaranteed access to the boardroom again reiterate the idea that there is an 'ideal' and that because he has senior business experience, he should be able to find roles very easily and that the barrier is boards or headhunters not being able to 'make the connection' between his experience and what they are looking for. This is similar to Martin's account presented earlier, where his difficulty is attributed to his not previously being a CFO or CEO: the implication is that he would be a good director and is suited for the role but that boards are looking for narrow or specific kinds of experience and cannot see how his experience 'translates' into that.

SCARLETT: So do you get any feedback about what experience you need to have?
DAVID [SECOND INTERVIEW]: THEY DON'T REALLY SPECIFY but I would read into their remarks, executive board experience. So, I've

got executive experience of running this company, which is a private company, but it's a company that turns over a billion and has 10,000 employees, so this is a big and successful business in its own right. So, I've worked at the top at executive board level within [company] but that doesn't carry as much weight as if I'd worked in a similar corporate of exactly the same size doing exactly the same thing with those magic letters 'plc' [publicly listed company] seem to count for something.

David similarly states that his experience is 'wrong' because boards are unable to see how his experience 'translates', despite meeting the high-status criteria that others have also cited.

What was striking about the interviews with those people who felt they had the wrong experience was how often they referred to this as a translation problem: the board's or headhunters' inability to recognise the candidates' experience as being suitable rather than there being other issues with bias in the appointment process. This is notable because it still implies that those who have the right experience will find it easy rather than, for instance, treating this as evidence that the selection process is not based solely on experience. It provides a framework for candidates to describe their struggle to get board roles without challenging their conviction in their own ability, as their seniority and suitability for roles is not brought into question, and without challenging the focus on the right experience.

SCARLETT: What is it about yourself that you feel that you have to get across when you're going for these positions?

JAMES [FIRST INTERVIEW]: That I am not a lawyer *per se*, that I have been involved in the leadership management of a large international business that turns over 450 million, 4,000 people, that I have had leadership roles, and I've been involved in transformational change and have managed a variety of different projects. I was involved as well as six partners in the integration board of the firm when we came together financially in the 2000s and that I'd been involved in these sort of things and not just been watching from the sidelines.

SCARLETT: Yeah, of course. And is the battle about being a lawyer something you'd faced already then?

JAMES: Nobody's put it to me expressly in an interview context, but I think that I've spent a lot of time thinking about what it is I can bring to bear and what it is that concerns people about lawyers. You know, risk averse, not challenging, that [sic] sort of issues.

James has a similar account as David and Peter, again emphasising that he has the 'right experience' much like that discussed at the beginning of the chapter but that he faces a difficulty in translating it to boards.

The belief that lawyers are not sought by boards because they are risk averse was mentioned by many of the interviewees and is worth examining further, given that it contradicts the literature that emphasises the value women can bring as directors because of their presumed risk aversion (Roberts, 2015; Prügl, 2015). This also discursively combines the right experience with the *right personality* discourse (discussed later in this chapter), connecting objective and subjective criteria in a way that upholds a view of the process as objective and rational: in this account, lawyers can be legitimately rejected because of their personality traits under the objective criterion of their industry background.

Candidates from human resources (HR) backgrounds described similar difficulties:

CATRIN [FIRST INTERVIEW]: I got called about a FTSE 250 one, went to see the headhunter. They were very positive and said they'll be in touch. Then they didn't kind of get back to me; then I spoke to them and said, you know, 'What's happening?' And they said, "Oh they've changed their spec; they don't want anybody with a HR background anymore" because the general view is an HR background is not popular.

Similarly to Martin earlier, Catrin suggests that anything which is not seen as part of the core business, such as HR and legal, are constructed as less desired, in this case from advice she was given from a headhunter, as an explanation for her being turned down for a role. The notion that on this occasion the board changed its specification explains the board's decision to choose a different candidate, which discursively casts the process as rational and rigorous. That HR is 'not popular' is stated as if common sense and obvious. A general view that cannot be challenged by Catrin or the headhunter.

The 'Wild Card'

The pervasiveness of the right experience discourse also emerges in how those with the 'wrong' experience are described as 'wild cards'. Although not exclusively used by search firms, this is a common concept in their practice (cf. Faulconbridge *et al.*, 2009). Indeed, during the design of the research, the partner search firm recommended that we establish a sample from individuals with different industry backgrounds and include some 'wild cards'—i.e. those who did not fit into other categories. There were also many individuals who described being referred to, either by a board or a headhunter, as a 'wild card'.

ELEANOR [FIRST INTERVIEW]: So, I think that of the four people who were on the list (.) my understanding is that there were kind of two, what's the word? Kind of (.) tried and tested, establishment-type people, and then there were two slightly 'wild cards', and I was probably a wild card. And I think also at the end of the day, and I've (.) I mean (.) this is a generalisation, but there's been lots of anecdotal evidence that the boards, particularly listed companies, are quite risk averse when it comes to choosing their board members.

Here Eleanor is describing a time she was put forward for a role by a head-hunter and was not successful. She uses the term 'wild card' to describe her experience, placed in opposition to 'tried and tested establishment types', who by inference have the right experience to be on boards and are more likely to be chosen. This reproduces the idea of an ideal board member who has very specific experience that Eleanor does not have. As well as providing the 'right experience' discourse as an explanation for her lack of success, this also casts 'wild-card' candidates—those who do not have the right experience—as a 'risk' to the board, seeming to justify bias away from these individuals on the grounds of their reputational risk (Gaughan, 2013). Additionally, wild cards are a risk to the headhunter if they believe that the client is less likely to select them. It, therefore, makes more sense to them to fill the short and long list with candidates who are seen as less of a risk.

SARAH [FIRST INTERVIEW]: So [they] had said in the brief that they were looking for an Internet-experienced businessperson, preferably with marketing skills. They were interested in women because (.) well, (.) they did have one woman on the board, and they were willing to take someone who hadn't had prior board experience. So that, that's what we could term the 'wild card': the role that had more flexibility in it.

Here Sarah uses the term 'wild card' slightly differently to refer to a vacancy on the board that she was able to take with her background—in this case, her background in technology and marketing, being a woman and not having previous board experience. Her admission that the board was 'willing' to take a wild card also suggests a perceived negative atti-tude toward those individuals. While the 'wild-card' label is frequently used to describe individuals, Sarah's account suggests that boards and headhunters also use the term 'wild card' to describe certain *roles*, imply-ing that there are 'normal' roles for candidates with the right experience and wild card roles for other candidates, where they can be more flexible in the skills they are looking for.

Sarah's account also suggests that 'wild card' is a gendered term: in her case, being a woman contributed to her 'wild-card' status. Danielle also notes this, and she was highly critical of the gendered nature of being regarded as a wild card:

DANIELLE [FIRST INTERVIEW]: I mean headhunters will say, "We put you on as a wild card" and I'm like, "Wild card?" (.) It's not exactly (.)

I've had such a straightforward career. You just think, isn't that despicable to call (.) because you are a woman basically (.) a wild card? And you just think well if that's how they present you, For God's sake! "Oh, client, here's our list". And, "Oh, we've got this 'wild card' for you".

In her first interview, Danielle states specifically that she feels the wild card label is due to her being a woman; she also notes the potential negative discursive effect of the label and highlights how this might affect her likelihood of being appointed, as it sets her up as a candidate who boards may be less likely to choose and places her in direct opposition to candidates who are an easier choice.

She talks about this again in her second interview; between the first and second interview, she was appointed to a board and notes here how, before she had this experience, she 'used to' be described as a wild card:

DANIELLE [SECOND INTERVIEW]: I mean what they [headhunters] used to say (.), which slightly shocked me, is things like, "Oh no, you're the wild card". (.) Which used to (.) I can't remember who told me that, and I just said, THAT IS SHOCKING. I'm the most, you know, tradit- my experience is not at all off the- you know, sort of, wacky at all. I mean, you know, a wild card to me would be taking an artistic director and putting them forward for a regulated business, you know? Not a boring lawyer who's done loads on risk management. I am not considered by any stretch of my imagination a wild card. And yet, you know, that's how some of them have described me on the basis that their clients come along with a very prescriptive brief which doesn't envisage a woman to starters usually, or a lawyer, and all this kind of stuff. So what they've said sometimes is "we put your name forward for the longlist, but the client takes it off".

Again, Danielle notes how she 'used to' be referred to as a wild card, something she believes is due to her being a woman and a lawyer and, therefore, has the 'wrong experience'. She is explicit about the damaging consequences of this kind of discourse: the 'wild-card' label portrays the candidate as a risk, an unlikely sell or a less desirable candidate before he or she even gets to the board interview. Like other areas where the right experience discourse emerges, this is connected in her discourse with the headhunters' need to categorise candidates within their industry background, something that can be seen as a product of the practice of search firms (Faulconbridge *et al.*, 2009) as well as board composition.

We have seen that ideas of what constitutes an ideal board member pervade the appointment process and are used in how the candidates explain their experience of the process, their career backgrounds, their motivations for seeking board roles and how they attribute their success and failure. These ideas are consistent: the 'ideal' has significant, high-level board experience, ideally with a plc. Those who feel they have similar or relevant experience frequently noted a need to 'translate': persuade boards that their experience is relevant, while those with the 'wrong experience' talk about being described both by boards and headhunters as a 'wild card'.

The Right Personality

As well as having the right experience, candidates emphasised the importance of having the right interpersonal skills, natural disposition or personality to be a good director. This too, forms part of the ideal board member.

MARTHA [FIRST INTERVIEW]: I'm used to making high-level decision making. Once you've been [states her role title], then you get comfortable making big strategic decisions based on partial information, you get used to using influencing skills (. . .) the business world is very much one of enquiry and influence, and that is really more my kind of natural posture.

To make sense of her suitability for boards, Martha draws on a 'right personality' discourse, relating this to her current role and describing it as her 'natural posture' (i.e. something she is 'naturally' suited to). She cites her experience of high-level strategic decisions, similar to the career narratives discussed earlier, and connects this to intangible or unmeasurable personality traits, which she states are central to the 'business world' and her 'natural posture'.

SCARLETT: And what do you think makes you suitable for board roles?
LINDA [FIRST INTERVIEW]: First of all, I think it's (.) you cannot be a risk manager without being a curious person. Curiosity and challenge, I suppose, go with risk management.

Linda's focus on being curious and able to challenge the board also draws on this discourse of having the 'right personality', again emphasising highly subjective and individual traits or preferences and connecting them to her previous experience. The notion of 'challenging' the board was particularly common in candidates' accounts, and this likely reflects the wider expectations of the role of the non-executive, who is expected to monitor the executives and challenge them if necessary (FRC, 2018). This wider discourse is a way for candidates to make sense of how they see themselves in relation to the ideal and part of the discursive construction of the ideal board member.

GARY [THIRD INTERVIEW]: The one thing you need is courage; it's about personality. It's the courage to say, "No. I don't understand that".

Or, "Run that past me again". Or, "No, I actually disagree with that!" And (.) that's a real hallmark.

Gary's statement offers another example of how the ability to challenge is drawn on as part of the discursive construction of the ideal board member. Although the 'need to challenge' was found in both men's and women's accounts, it is interesting from a gendered perspective, given the wider literature on leadership and the difficulties that women are presumed to face when needing to challenge without being seen as aggressive. The examples he provides of how directors can challenge (used here, we can assume, to show how *he* can challenge) are direct statements of disagreement stated assertively and could be seen as combative; it is notable that this is how he performs (literally demonstrating in the research interview) how directors need to be.

That 'challenge' (something that directors have to *do*) is connected with 'courage' (something that directors have to *be or have*) is also reminiscent of neoliberal (feminist) discourses (Adamson and Kelan, 2019), where the assertion is made that, provided an individual has enough courage and internalised conviction, they will necessarily be able to challenge the board. There is, therefore, a discursive muddling and amalgamation of experience and subjectivity evident throughout candidates' descriptions of the ideal board member, building a picture of what good directors need to do, be and have while drawing on a rhetoric of meritocracy, objectivity and neoliberal feminist discourses.

SCARLETT: What is it that you think your key strengths [are], and why you've got the positions you've got so far, and what will get you the positions in the future?

RACHEL [FIRST INTERVIEW]: I think enormous inquisitiveness, [being] very open-minded and willing to explore and understand where people are coming from but then also with a lot of business judgement, all probably quite strong. We've just done the board review [and], I was described as a nice attack dog HEHE. So the ability to explore, enquire, understand, probe. Linked to that is some courage, being willing to name things that are a concern and not just go with the flow.

Rachel's description of what traits makes a good board member draw on the same 'ability to challenge' discourse but using different discursive repertoires to 'perform' or place herself in the role. She highlights curiosity, the intellectual challenge of the role and business judgement, and like Gary earlier, she states that good directors have to have courage to challenge the decisions of the board. In her account, however, she describes this as being 'willing to name things that are a concern', a markedly less combative account of being able to challenge the board. This is validated further by her description in the board evaluation as a 'nice attack dog', which represents a narrative resource that she uses in order to highlight her ability: to demonstrate that she is able to challenge the board while also being 'nice'.

Rachel's account is also an example of how subjective and objective criteria are discursively combined: she asserts aspects of herself that are highly subjective and internalised (inquisitiveness, open-mindedness) as fundamental to the role, presenting them as abilities or skills and, therefore, as something that an 'objective' appointment process would need to look for. She also combines 'business judgement' with her ability to understand people's perspectives—a trait often associated with women leaders (Eagly and Carli, 2003) and frequently related to an internalised subjectivity or natural ability, rather than something demonstrated through having the 'right experience'.

LINDA: [FIRST INTERVIEW]: [I think it's] the opportunity to look at how other people run things and see where the, you know, the potential pitfalls are, look at the strategy, see if it's well thought through. The opportunity [to] (.) in effect do, in a somewhat lower key fashion, the type of activity which I do and have done full on for the past 20-odd years in risk: pulling things apart intellectually to look at whether they stand up to examination and then raising questions and encouraging debate about the areas which are somewhat suspect. I have spent my life, effectively, in this sort of car mechanics' equivalent of stripping the engine down, before putting it back together and finding out whether I've left any screws missing on the way.

Linda similarly draws on the 'right personality' discourse, and in describing how her personal traits make her suited to boards, she provides her career experience as evidence. In a similar way to Rachel, she describes challenging the board as an intellectual or cerebral activity through assessing the company, raising questions and encouraging debate rather than being combative and directly 'challenging' the decisions. This suggests ways in which these women are seen to be doing gender 'well and differently' (Mavin and Grandy, 2012) through negotiating masculine and feminine leadership traits in order to highlight how they are good directors. Asked what would make him a good board director, Benjamin responds as follows:

BENJAMIN [SECOND INTERVIEW]: Well, obviously being able to fool some of the people all of the time is important; that's been my, that's my career motto anyway. (.) To be honest with you, I mean, I must have intelligence, I'm interested, I'm interested, (.) I care about the companies I'm on the boards of (. . .). I'M QUITE A SOCIABLE PERSON. I get on with people quite well (.), that's is one of my personality traits really. (.) I can turn the charm on when I need to or turn it off.

I would say, [a] slightly theatrical approach to life (.) no bad thing really; [a] measure of cynicism (.) is important I think (. . .). I think anybody who is ANY bloody good will have all those traits. And absent one or more of them, you're a deficient director. (.) Just like with a lawyer, there's no bloody law in the world if you can't persuade somebody to listen to you.

Benjamin similarly recounts what he sees as being the personality and character of a good director and draws on similar personalised criteria: an ability to be sociable, curiosity, passion for the businesses he works with and a degree of cynicism, which he states are essential traits that have made him successful. This is, again, individualised: he takes aspects of his own subjectivity and relates it to what he thinks boards need while casting them as necessary traits that have to be brought to the boardroom by each individual member. This discourse also acts as a way for him to claim agency where the discourse is related to success or something positive. This was seen throughout, where candidates, particularly men, adopt individualised discourses to account for their success and attribute failure to outside forces (we return to this later in the book). In this narrative construction, there is also little space for variation on boards; rather, certain candidates—i.e. those who are *like him*—are well suited to the role, while others are not.

When describing how their personality fits the criteria that boards need, interviewees also often accompanied this with an example or 'evidence' that they possess these personality traits, typically tied to having the right experience. In Rachel's account, for example, the anecdote of her being described as a 'nice attack dog' in the board evaluation is used to demonstrate that she has the right personal traits to be a director; similarly, Linda refers to herself as a car mechanic with a background in risk; Benjamin, after stating what he feels are the crucial personality traits, reiterates that this is a skill that lawyers (i.e. him) have, using his career background as confirmation that he has the 'right' personality to be a good director.

The Right Fit

Much of the literature surrounding the non-executive director and boards discusses fit with the board, and this is often offered as an explanation for a lack of diversity on boards. We found much evidence to support this, alongside a problematic relationship with 'fit'—namely, evidence that describes 'fit with the board' as a crucial part of what makes them credible.

SCARLETT: What is it that you think you personally would have to bring to the board? What would be your strengths?

RAYMOND [FIRST INTERVIEW]: I think a number of things. One is, I think, an ability to feel comfortable in a board, in those conversations. I know how it operates. Getting along with other board members: that's effectively my technical specialism.

In stating how he is suited to board roles, Raymond emphasises his ability to get on with other directors, presenting that as crucial to being a good director. As in the earlier accounts where candidates describe their personalities and how they are suitable for boards, 'getting along' with other directors, 'feeling comfortable' in a board and knowing 'how it [a board] operates' are described as abilities or 'technical specialisms', drawing on objective or rational language to describe something highly subjective. His euphemistic references to 'those' conversations or knowing how 'it' operates also hints that boards are spaces that have a specific way of being and modes of interaction rather than just needing to get along generally.

SCARLETT: And why do you think that's important to get along with the other board members?
SIMON [SECOND INTERVIEW]: It just makes it more interesting. A more interesting conversation with a person who is more animated, got lots of experience in lots of different (.) it's a much more interesting conversation than a dull person who might have a huge amount up here [points to his head], but can't quite get it out (.) Boards need, boards work best when they're an organic whole.

Earlier in the interview, Simon had stated that it is important for directors to get along with each other, and when asked why, his explanation presents the board as a whole unit ('an organic whole') and that this group 'getting along' is an important part of the role. This emphasises the informality of directors' work and describes an effective board as one that has 'interesting' discussions. He then contrasts this with the notion that directors need to have a specific and narrow type of experience instead arguing that directors need to come from a broad background in order to stimulate an interesting discussion.

Asked what type of NED Tom would want to recruit to a board he is already on, he states the following:

TOM: Well, you want people who are (.) who are intelligent, talkative (.) inspirational. I'd want all NEDs who'd stretch me if I were an executive and challenge me; who every time I went to a board meeting would come up with a new idea. Who looked at things differently. I don't want a bunch of failed or ex-CEOs doing, second-guessing me on, from a narrow base (. . .). I want a light cast from a different point of view that throws a different shadow, ^that's what I like to have happen on boards^ (. . .). Intellectual fun, intellectual fun as well, you know? Intellectually stimulating. You should come out feeling slightly exhausted because your brain has had to work. These are my perfect board meeting[s], you know.

Tom's description of the criteria required for a successful candidate is highly informal and subjective, pointing to interpersonal skills and a high-level intellectual ability to explain what the 'ideal' candidate should be. He had previously mentioned his conviction that directors meetings should be thought of more like dinner parties than work environments and uses this to support his description of the ideal board member and who he would want to be on his (hypothetical) board. Thus he directly challenges the idea that having the right experience is a good predictor for being a good director through his negative comments about ex-CEOs and instead emphasises the importance of intellectual and interpersonal skills.

These discourses also emerge in how directors discuss interviewing for roles.

KAREN [SECOND INTERVIEW]: So you get a call from the headhunter; then the chairman or chairwoman will typically meet you. Then he'll say, he will make a judgement, or she will make a judgement about whether or not they are, whether you will fit in. Because there is a dynamic to a board that is important, that isn't important on the executive side. The board is a collective beast—albeit that individuals are expected to express, challenge and all the other things, and they will be from different backgrounds—but if they are dysfunctional together, that is not a board. So the chairman is quite pivotal here.

In Karen's description, the same emphasis is evoked as in Tom's statement, where she describes the board as a whole ('a collective beast') and states that the most important aspect of being a good director is fitting in. This has two implications: fit with the board is used as a way to justify the primacy of the chair in deciding who to appoint, who determines an individuals' value as a director solely on his or her fit with the other members of the board and by inference is permitted to determine an individuals' ability as a director *solely* on these criteria. Karen also discursively downplays individual traits as a measure for suitability—e.g. the ability to challenge the board and express an opinion—and places the focus on the board functioning as a whole. This, therefore, justifies a process that could be seen as problematic or un-meritocratic—namely, a chair-led decision focused on fit with the board—on meritocratic terms. The dynamic of the board is, discursively at least, made more important than the value of the individual board members in the case of both success and failure.

In a later interview, Karen similarly describes the interview process when going for a board role, in this case for a role that she was successfully appointed to.

SCARLETT: What did you talk about in that initial meeting?
KAREN [THIRD INTERVIEW]: It was wide-ranging. What were my views on the challenges of the day? How should they be thinking about them? So they want to have your views on things; they want to know if you understand what's going on in the industry; they want to get a sense of what sort of personality you've got; they want to get a sense of whether you'll rub along well with the others, so there's a combination of different things.

Again, in this extract, she focuses on the board needing to establish how well she will 'rub along with' the other members of the board, whether she has the right personality and opinions around the issues the board is facing and that this is decided by the chair. She notes the informality of the interview but does not explicitly challenge it, and it is instead presented as important areas of assessment for the appointing board.

When interviewing for board roles, all candidates met with the chair of the board, but it is also common for them to meet with other members of the board.

LINDA [SECOND INTERVIEW]: So then I met with each of them [other board members]. They obviously tried to do the same as the chairman did, trying to gauge whether they could work with me, whether they felt I had the right skill set, and everyone's different. Take for instance [name]. I met him outside the offices. And he and I spent an hour and a half raging about regulators, you know? And about this and that, we had a debate! And he said at the end, he said, "OH, I thoroughly enjoyed that!" HEHE. It was, it's about (.) what do you bring to the table?

When Linda met with another director of the board whom she was later successful in gaining, she described the importance of both having the right skill set and getting along with the other board members. This combines highly subjective assessment criteria with more objective criteria and prioritises both in the construction of an ideal board member. In this account, the importance of 'fit' between her and the directors is again emphasised.

Although the majority of the interviews in the research focused on the individuals' own experiences of trying to get onto boards, one interview with a candidate who had been successful provided an insight into what this looked like from the point of view of an appointing board. In this case, the shortlist was all women, and he described why he felt they had appointed the successful candidate:

SCARLETT: So were they all relatively similar in terms of their backgrounds, or were they completely different?

SIMON [THIRD INTERVIEW]: Different. [Name] comes from the marketing, human marketing side (.) Another lady that came from big, big corporate strategic side and then there was kind of entrepreneur-cum-big corporate (.) from actually outside the UK (. . .). And really you could have, I could have any three of them, all three of them frankly. In turn, they all provided something to the company.

SCARLETT: So what do you think pipped the one that you chose above the others?

SIMON: I think there was a certain (.) ease; ease and ability to get on with the executive is very important. (.) Also, I thought that she was quite resilient, coming to a (.) you know a [industry] culture with some measure of (.) self-confidence and not at all arrogant either. The other two candidates were intellectually very impressive, but she is as bright as them, but they came across as more intellectually combative, and although you need that sometimes, I think that maybe this particular CEO we have who's newish to the job (.) he needs a DIFFERENT KIND OF SUPPORT.

Although not the intended research focus, Simon's account of how another NED was chosen highlights many of the issues with the appointment process identified in this chapter. First, he demonstrates the contradictory narratives that are used around having the right experience: while candidates presume that they need to have highly specific kinds of experience, the shortlist in this case comprises three women with very different backgrounds who could all bring value to the board. While they presumably needed the background to be of a certain level of seniority (although this is not known from this extract), the specific industry background is not crucial to their likelihood of success.

Simon's account also highlights the emphasis on fit with the board, where the successful candidate was chosen because of her 'ability' to get along with the members of the executive team, something that, in this extract, is presented as more important than her specific experience background. It also highlights how having the right personality might be enacted in the process, where her self-confidence (notable that it comes 'without arrogance') is treated as an asset; similarly, this notes how directors need to be able to challenge the board without being 'too' challenging. This is not to regard Simon's account as being a neutral, accurate description of exactly what 'happened'; rather, it suggests how 'fit with the board' and having the 'right personality' are discourses mobilised in the appointment process, while having the 'right' experience discourses are stronger when candidates are in the early stages of the process: as a door opener. This extract suggests then that having the right personality and fitting with the board is highly influential at interview stages.

Or Fitting In?

While the need to fit with the board was a common discourse throughout the interviews, a contributing discourse of 'fitting in' was used by several women when accounting for their appearance and how to 'fit' with other directors in boardrooms.

SARAH [SECOND INTERVIEW]: I don't really think it's (.) I think as long as you're ticking the hygiene factors, and you're the right sort of candidate with the right sort of experience (.) and then when you show up to the interview you look something like this [refers to own appearance]. (. . .) You know, I tend not to do anything that is overly going to be (.) a reason or an excuse for someone to go OH, MY GOD she's got pink nails. I do think because particularly FTSE and AIM-listed [Alternative Investment Market] chair people are pretty conservative. They are thinking of a number of things; they're not just thinking about "will you fit in with the board? Do you know your stuff? Will you make a great contribution?" They're also thinking, 'How is the market going to react?' You know, "What's this person going to look like, be like, behave like when I roll them out in front of the exec?"

Sarah's account here is a response to a wider discussion we were having about the extent to which she feels that candidates can prepare for their interviews with chairs and boards; she suggests that it is not easy, appropriate or, perhaps, that it is not necessary to overly prepare for interviews. The way she describes the process draws on the experience discourse described earlier, where passing the 'hygiene factors' means being deemed to have the right experience and references before the interview takes place. She also relates the preparation for interviews to concern with her appearance, something we had discussed earlier on in the interview briefly, and here describes how she would prepare for the interview in terms of having the right appearance and clothing in order to 'fit in' with the board.

CATRIN [FIRST INTERVIEW]: A female headhunter, she's quite senior, well-known in the headhunting world on board searches, and she sat there and she basically said that if you are going for any interview as a woman, then you must make sure, before you go, that you must have your hair blown dry. And that you must, because you're trying to market yourself to old men, you must try and look like their wives. Imagine! I thought, that's really demeaning, fancy saying that. I don't usually wear a lot of make-up and then I thought perhaps I should be HEHE.

While some women, like Sarah, discussed their appearance as a choice they made, some stated that they had been advised to consider their appearance for the appointment process. Catrin, described advice she (and other women) had been given from a headhunter at an event for women seeking board roles. The emphasis that Catrin places on the headhunter being senior and well-known is also relevant because she holds a position of relative power and can, therefore, offer advice and be a transmitter for these discourses. It is notable that the headhunter in question attributes this to the men on the board: there is no clear explanation as to why these men would be more inclined to hire women who look like their wives, but this has sexual undertones, an inherent focus on women's appearance and a perpetuation of discourses being presented as factual, despite being at best biased and at worst sexist.

ISABEL [FIRST INTERVIEW]: You also need to understand the world and the language and the nuances and the culture, and you've got to fit in. So I had a session with [a communications coach] in August in terms of just clarifying what I wanted to do, and she is looking at my hair and says, "Oh gosh. Start looking at all the women you want to be, the NEDs; you might have to cut it, or you might have to get it blow dried every time you want to do something", and I was like, "Oh, but this is my identity!" Gosh, this is going on tape, and this is terrible, but it would be interesting to see, because I guess I don't (.), do I come for one [sic]? I had a very successful career and people knew who I was, and they knew that I'd get the job done. So, I guess, in a different world, I always like to go bright colours, so am I not your typical (.) banker person? I mean her advice was, "Okay you might have to be that little bit more muted"; that's probably the nicest way to say it, "and more polished in terms of how you present yourself".

In this extract, Isabel outlines the importance of 'fitting in' with the board, and needing to look right when doing so, as part of her preparation for seeking board roles. It is notable that she compares this with her previous (full-time, senior position) role where she felt more able to express her personality through her dress and appearance while feeling that, by contrast, the non-executive recruitment process required her to look a certain way that is more conservative and muted than she has been previously. Like Sarah's description of boards as highly conservative spaces, Isabel attributes this as being due to 'the world and the language and the nuances and the culture' [of boards] and needing to fit in with that culture; this is bound up in 'looking good and sounding right' (Warhurst and Nickson, 2007: p. 2) for the role.

The concept of 'fit' and its potential to affect who is chosen for board roles has been suggested by others, often with the presumption that it will exclude women from the boardroom. In these accounts, we see how this exclusion may work in practice, where women in the research describe concern with ensuring that they fit with the board. The language they use also suggests a concern with 'fitting in' by ensuring that their appearance is congruent with the culture of the board. This, in part, means downplaying femininity: a way for them to do gender 'differently' by putting forward a conservative, muted and at times literally greyer version of themselves. It is notable, however, that this is rarely discussed in explicit gendered terms; instead, it is attributed to the conservative nature of boards and the perceived risk of appointing a director who does not fit (in). It is also notable, although perhaps not surprising, that no men in the research talked about ensuring that their appearance was right for fitting in with the board.

Conclusion

This chapter has outlined how, throughout the interviews with aspirant directors, we can see a discursive construction of the ideal board member manifest in peoples' accounts. This is made up of three key aspects: having the right experience, the right personality and fitting with the board. This construction is important because it demonstrates how a preference for these kinds of experience can be embedded in the appointment process but without necessarily supporting a meritocratic route to success. By placing emphasis on these three criteria of experience, personality and fit, it presents an overall discourse that asserts that individuals fitting this ideal will be appointed and reiterates a meritocratic model of appointments that does not occur in practice. We have also seen how this construction is gendered.

Throughout the interviews, candidates describe or refer to their qualifications for board roles by drawing on a 'right experience' discourse, outlining the importance of having the right experience for the role. These assertions tie to the wider literature that draws on a human capital explanation for the lack of women on boards. This discourse was particularly strong in those who come from backgrounds that are more typically seen on boards, such as having been a CFO, having held previous board roles or having worked in banking or risk (Sealy and Doherty, 2012; Lowe *et al.*, 2015, 2016, 2017) and who saw their experience as leading naturally to a board role. Those from other backgrounds also drew on this discourse in their career narratives, placing their experience in similar discursive terms. When asked what makes them suitable, candidates drew on elements of elite identity: they frequently mention markers of their elite status, pointing to their experience as senior executives and directors, awards or markers of significance or 'unique' or rare position. All candidates explained how they were ideal for director work by drawing on their experience and locating it within this elite identify framework.

Supplementing the 'right experience' discourse was a strong idea around what constituted the 'wrong experience'. Candidates from certain career backgrounds (most notably law, large professional services or accountancy firms and HR) described how they were told by headhunters or other people in their networks that they would find it difficult to become a director because it was assumed that they had the wrong experience; they have career backgrounds that are seen as less desirable by boards. They described the frustration they felt in translating their experience into what boards are looking for: going through discursive work to describe how their backgrounds were more aligned with the 'right experience' by emphasising their seniority and elite status and their previous board work or insisting that they are different than the typical candidates from their backgrounds. This represents a kind of discursive 'othering' and dis-identification, which relies upon and reproduces the emphasis on having the right experience.

Despite the strength of the right experience discourse, throughout the research (as in the wider literature), there was little consistency or a direct, clear relationship between experience and success. Having the 'right experience' is not necessarily a clear route to becoming a director. Rather than treating this as evidence for a preference for those kinds of experience, as has been the case in other similar research (e.g. Sealy and Doherty, 2012; Sheridan and Milgate, 2005), we can understand this as an interpretive repertoire that candidates use to make sense of the process in the interviews and come from wider discourses. Candidates frequently draw on external factors to offer evidence for boards requiring specific kinds of experience; market discourses, research reports, social changes or headhunters' feedback are all used as evidence to confirm why there is a preference for these areas of experience. The strength of these discourses and our interest in them as researchers, therefore, lie in their reproductive effect: reiterating the notion that boards require the right experience (and that candidates with the wrong experience, often women, will find it difficult to get roles) reproduces the idea that these experiences are prerequisites, even when this is not necessarily seen in reality.

Another discourse that emerged in candidates' accounts of the ideal board member was having the 'right' personality traits. These were often broad and wide-ranging but centred around being comfortable making high-level decisions, being curious and enjoying intellectual problems and being able to challenge the board. In the wider literature, it is suggested that this may be an area where gender bias occurs: it is presumed that women are less able to challenge and influence the board than men or that they do it in different ways through flattery, higher interpersonal skills or emotional intelligence (Westphal, 2010). There is evidence to suggest that 'challenge' is a gendered concept: when describing how they 'did' challenge (frequently described as something 'done') men more frequently gave active accounts, while women drew on less active discourses, emphasising intellectual or questioning aspects rather than direct disagreement with directors. This may indicate areas where women are doing gender 'well and differently' (Mavin and Grandy, 2012), taking on the need to challenge as part of the director role but doing it in a less combative way than their male counterparts.

That said, the similarities between men's and women's discussions of the right personality were far more common than their differences: the personality traits required related strongly to the kinds of traits discussed in the literature, emphasising directors' independence and ability to challenge the board. There was also little evidence of women adopting more 'feminine' kinds of leadership in order to get roles, problematising the notion that boards are looking for traits typically associated with women directors or women leaders and further implying that individuals need to fit a model of governance that is already established. This was further evidenced by the negative connotations candidates gave to 'risk aversion', a trait commonly attributed to women and often used to justify a business case for women on boards (Roberts, 2015) but here seen as a barrier. Risk aversion is treated as something abject or undesired; often, directors from these backgrounds would work to place their experience in more business-led terms, identifying themselves away from the 'typical' lawyer, for instance. Overall, this suggests first that the business case for women on boards has had little effect in persuading boards that they need 'feminine' leaders and second that board members—both men and women—have to display traits which fit into those already desired by the board.

A third discourse that emerged in candidates' accounts was the perceived need for directors to 'fit with the board'. This discourse emphasises the need for directors to get along with other board members; often, candidates referred to boards as collectives or as an 'organic whole', where getting along with each other is seen as a prerequisite to a successful board. They also frequently emphasised the informality of boards, describing effective boards as 'dinner parties' with interesting or intellectual discussions rather than as a space where things are 'done'. Other research (Doldor *et al.*, 2012; Pye, 2000, 2002) has suggested that 'fit with the board' is a prerequisite for directors joining boards; however, this also suggests that even aspirant directors (including those it may disadvantage, such as women or those from atypical backgrounds) still draw on this discourse, justifying and reproducing it, and suggesting that they have a personal invested interest in it. This construction often operates as an explanation (implicitly or explicitly) for an informal appointment system, which judges the potential success of directors according to their personalities and how they fit with other directors', and aligns subjective assessment criteria with objective assessment processes.

Under a similar rubric to 'fit' with the board, there emerged a highly gendered discourse of 'fitting in' present in women's accounts when discussing their appearance, dress and aesthetic presences. This discourse draws heavily on notions of respectable business femininity (Mavin and Grandy, 2012), where we see women's concern with dressing appropriately and achieving respectable business femininity in order to be evaluated as credible leaders and potential directors. This again is an area where we see the reproduction of discourses from external sources: women frequently mentioned advice they had been given by colleagues, friends or headhunters about how to 'look good and sound right' (Warhurst and Nickson, 2007) for director roles. This was often attributed to boards being 'conservative' and concerned with reputation (Gaughan, 2012), downplaying the potential for criticism. The need for women to 'fit in' was also often described in neoliberal feminist terms and presented as a way for women to learn how to 'play the game'. Even when women were critical of needing to dress according to the rules of business femininity, it is seen as an unavoidable part of the process, with a kind of resigned irony.

This chapter also suggests how discourses around the ideal board member are upheld and reproduced in candidates' interactions with other people. This is highly common in their interactions with headhunters, supporting wider research that suggests headhunters have an effect on how the 'ideal' candidate is viewed (Coverdill and Finlay, 1998; Finlay and Coverdill, 2007; Faulconbridge *et al.*, 2009; Wirz, 2014). Candidates frequently offered anecdotes of cases where headhunters stated that their experience or 'credentials' are in high demand or that they fitted a client brief; they use this as a resource in the research interviews to evidence a focus on the right experience. This, therefore, has a truth effect: by being offered as 'evidence', headhunters are discursively cast as experts and afforded power to dictate what the ideal is. The focus on having the right experience is reproduced and reiterated. Throughout the interviews, candidates mention areas where headhunters are seen to dictate the discourse: stating that previous board experience is a prerequisite, using the 'wrong experience' as a reason for a candidate being rejected and describing candidates as 'wild cards'. In research into headhunters' practices around board diversity, Doldor and colleagues point to the inherently gendered quality of these descriptive hierarchies. They found cases of women seeking roles being described as 'lateral suggestions' or 'marginal' when they do not meet the 'standard' profile in terms of their experience (Doldor *et al.*, 2016: p. 296). Indeed, the frequency with which headhunters are mentioned alongside the discourses around having the right or wrong experience may indicate the effect they have in reproducing these discourses. It should also be noted that often the right experience was related to the candidate fitting the 'brief' for a role, suggesting, as research into headhunters more widely does (Faulconbridge *et al.*, 2009; Wirz, 2014), that a narrow client brief is a significant barrier or gateway to board roles.

The discourses that make up the construction of the ideal board member can be seen as operating as impression management (Westphal, 2010) that acts to uphold directors' elite status, power and influence. As Westphal (2010) suggests in his commentary on corporate directors' job descriptions as impression management, they present themselves in a way that 'conform[s] to the normative expectations and interests of powerful constituents, in order to enhance the legitimacy of the position within those constituents, and thus secure access to resources for themselves, their group or organization' (Westphal, 2010: p. 320). By doing so, they implicitly justify the need for an elite appointment process or 'closure mechanism' for entry onto boards by upholding directors as members of the corporate elite. Describing the ideal board member as someone with specific or unique, elite experience; the right personality; the ability to challenge other directors; and the ability to 'fit' and 'fit in' with the board constructs an individual whose elite position is justified while locating themselves within it.

The use of these discourses also has the discursive effect of presenting the appointment process as rational and meritocratic by foregrounding experience, personality and fit with the board as vital entry requirements. These requirements are also impervious to critique because of the relative flexibility in what makes a good director (see, for example, Westphal, 2010). The impossibility of having (at all times) the right experience, right personality and fit with the board means that candidates can draw on any aspect of their identities and place it within both an elite identity framework and a meritocratic one. Even when discussing areas of unfairness or potential bias in the process (such as the emphasis on certain kinds of experience or difficulties faced by those from the wrong background or needing to fit in with the board), this still supports discourses of meritocracy through its lack of challenge of the process or how it operates. In this way, even while they are challenging the system of director appointments, candidates discursively maintain it.

Notes

1. All names throughout are pseudonyms.
2. Another interviewee, who had put me in touch with him.

4   The Art of Networking

Non-executive director recruitment is characterised by its opacity and reliance on recommendations, personal networks and reputation (Doldor *et al.*, 2012; EHRC, 2016; Gaughan, 2013). As a result, understanding networks and networking is crucial to unlocking how the appointment process may be biased towards men or discourage candidates who are not already in director networks. In this chapter, we explore how aspirant directors go about seeking board roles, the discourses they use to account for their networking practices and how they gain and maintain visibility with 'gatekeepers' during the appointment process.

First, we demonstrate the priority given to networking in candidates' accounts and how they strategically gain visibility with gatekeepers. In describing this, candidates draw on two contrasting discourses: strategic networking and subtle networking. These are gendered because we find that women are less able to perform subtle networking as a route to success and feel a greater need to be strategic and put themselves forward. Second, we also outline how candidates bridge the gap between strategic and subtle networking through the use of recommendations and the importance they place on being recommended and recommending others. Third, we show how, as a result of the imperative to recommend and be recommended, networking occurs within and produces gendered spaces: women more commonly describe recommending other women as a way to tackle the male-dominated 'Old Boys' networks while also being highly critical of women-only networks and networking events. Men rarely discussed equivalent formal networking, and the majority of their networking is informal and one-on-one. This suggests that women's networks may be spatially ghettoised away from individuals with the power to appoint directors. These findings together suggest both that women's networks are different and that their networking is different, making it more difficult to get access to roles.

Strategic Networking

From very early on in the research—even before the research interviews had started—it was clear that networking was regarded as the main, if not the sole, route to the boardroom. This was clear in the interviews where it was treated as a given that looking for roles meant networking with non-executive directors and headhunters.

SCARLETT: So, with the non-executive positions, how have you gone about starting that search?

LINDA [FIRST INTERVIEW]: I have become a complete CV tart. I think is the answer to that! HEHE. No, I know a lot of people in the board practices anyway. Ironically, the GroupBank diaspora is amazing. A lot of people who have left GroupBank went into executive search. So I know three or four of the senior people at different board risk practices; I've been to see them. I've also been to see the other search agents and introduced myself to their board practices. I've just basically, you know, cold-called and marketed, said, "I want to come and see you; this is what I want to do", just basically get on their radar. (.) I've then drawn up a list of everybody that I know who is already a non-exec (.), and I've been to see all of them.

As in Linda's account here, candidates frequently answered questions about their search for board roles by describing how they had gone about their networking, and often the two were conflated, suggesting that they were seen as the same thing and that networking is seen as the primary way to get a board role (see also Brown *et al.*, 2016) because such roles are not publicly advertised. The way Linda describes her networking is typical of many candidates' accounts: it is a strategic and targeted process; she initiates contact with as many people in her network as possible in order to gain visibility (as Linda describes it, to get 'on their radar') with people who may be able to give them access to boards—most commonly current NEDs and headhunters, particularly those who work in 'board practices'—dedicated board-level recruitment.

Understandably, the breadth of an individuals' network and the proximity to current non-executive directors was a significant factor in how easy they felt this initial stage of networking was. In Linda's case, her previous career had afforded her access to many people who were now headhunters specialising in board appointments. Linda's use of the term 'ironically' is interesting in this context: it could be interpreted as a way to downplay how her previous role in a bank has given her access to people currently in board roles or search firms; there is nothing especially ironic about the seniority of her network, but 'irony' seems to describe it as a kind of lucky coincidence rather than due to her position within an elite corporate network.

NICHOLAS [FIRST INTERVIEW]: So I really started at that beginning phase with building my networks up. So in my 100-day plan, I set myself the target of a hundred contacts in a hundred days. These were contacts that divided into four categories really: former colleagues, good friends, headhunters and business contacts or former clients. I had a lot of business cards and names on business cards, but these people that I never really thought about in the past as being potential leverage points for me. So I parked myself in the [members club], and sometimes I would have five meetings a day. And the law of network dynamics actually works; so quite often, you meet somebody they don't necessarily provide a 'happy coincidence' for you, but they give you the name and introduce you to somebody else (. . .); it was like a job; I went to work every day.

Nicholas similarly describes his networking as highly strategic: once he had decided he wanted to seek non-executive director roles he set himself a target of achieving a hundred new contacts in a hundred days. When I asked why he had chosen a hundred days, he explained that it had been common practice in his work as a consultant to set a hundred-day time limit on expected outcomes. This hints again at a tendency amongst candidates to draw on their previous career experience in order to explain the networking strategies they used or use repeated resources. It could also be a reference to the oft-cited 'first hundred days in office' (Ornstein and Schenkenberg, 1995, for instance) used to measure the success of a president or political leader during the time that his or her power and influence is at its greatest. The reference to 'leverage points' hints at a kind of commodification of relationships, where his contacts are seen as things to collect that have a clear use and aim rather than as affective or reciprocal relationships between people. Similar strategies were common in candidates' accounts: like Linda's mention of 'drawing up a list' of people, others described how they used spreadsheets to keep track of all the people they had contacted and when they had last made contact or using LinkedIn, a professional networking website, or BoardEx, a database of in-depth profiles and connections of business leaders, to establish who was connected to whom and to try to access them. This strategic networking discourse is also seen in how Nicholas sees networking as 'like a job', recognising networking as an active, deliberate process and as necessary *work* that has to be done in order to get a role, although while still ensuring to mention, by name, the private members club that he 'works' in; it is work, but it is elite work.

Similar to Linda, Nicholas's networking involved making contact with former colleagues and headhunters in order to increase the size of his network and look for people who can get him access to board roles. It is notable that he also states some of his contacts are 'good friends', blurring the boundary between social and business networking in a way that is often more common for men than women at senior levels (Mavin and Grandy, 2012). At the same time, even making contact with friends is discussed strategically and with the clear aim of broadening his networks by asking his contacts to introduce him to other contacts: the 'law of network dynamics'.

SARAH [FIRST INTERVIEW]: So I've been talking to all of the non-execs that I know. Some of the people here in [company] who know I'm retiring know some of the non-execs on other boards outside or in other firms and have put me in touch, and we've had conversations which have led to other introductions. It's been a bit like 'Pac-Man'.

Sarah similarly describes her networking as strategic and deliberate, with the clear aim of increasing the size of her network and gaining contact with other non-executive directors. The euphemisms and metaphors that candidates use to describe the process are also particularly evocative: Linda as becoming a 'CV tart', Nicholas as operating in the law of 'network dynamics' and Sarah as 'Pac-Man'. These metaphors suggest a range of different conceptions of networking that underpin their practices, drawing on similar discourses of strategic thinking and all with the overall aim of collecting or establishing as many relationships or connections as possible with those who might give them access to board roles.

The reliance on networks and networking to get roles was often implied rather than explicit: interviewees simply did not discuss any other way of getting roles. It was also notable that interviewees did not criticise this as much as we were perhaps expecting; rather, they were frustrated that they could not access the right people. There were some exceptions: occasions when interviewees stated specifically that this did not amount to a transparent process, despite a presumption that it is.

ALEXANDRA [THIRD INTERVIEW]: I don't think there is any two ways about it, because no matter how 'transparent', supposedly, the selection process is, it all comes back to personal recommendations and it all comes back to who you know. And I don't think there is any getting away from that. So in terms of "what do I need to do now?", I definitely need to go and look at all of the NEDs I know that I haven't contacted up to now and try to make contact with them.

Alexandra's account sums up the networking imperative perfectly and outlines explicitly that the process is reliant on networks and that this is a contradiction to an assumption that the process is transparent. This quote also highlights how the reliance on 'who you know' relates to being recommended, something we discuss later in this chapter. In Alexandra's quote, we can also see the dilemma that a networking imperative presents: while it is the only route to success, it is never truly finished; if the first round of networking does not lead to a role, candidates can only keep networking.

Subtle Networking

Alongside their descriptions of strategic networking, there emerged a contrasting but co-contributory discourse of *subtle networking*. Candidates emphasised the (need for) networking to be subtle, informal, non-deliberate and 'not pushy'.

GARY [FIRST INTERVIEW]: So what I did then was, I quietly just went to see a couple of headhunters that I had known. One or two had been friends, and others that I got an introduction to, and just said, "Look, this is what's been happening, and I just want to make sure that you know". I probably covered a dozen like that, a dozen of the top ones.

In this extract, Gary is describing how he went about networking and meeting with headhunters when he decided to retire from his executive role. While he, like everyone in the research, treats networking as the only route to the boardroom, he foregrounds this with subtle networking discourses: emphasising that he went to see headhunters 'quietly' to let them know he was retiring and looking for non-executive roles. It is also notable that he emphasises that the headhunters were friends, or he'd gained introductions from other people rather than cold-calling. This emphasises the informality as well as the closed nature of headhunters' networks but also highlights the seniority of his networks; he is able to see the top headhunters through this process.

SCARLETT: I mean, you said networking, so what does that involve for you?
IAN [FIRST INTERVIEW]: Just going to see people.
SCARLETT: And what sort of things have you been asking them?
IAN: Really (.) initially (.) letting them know that I'm looking and then keeping in touch to see if anything comes along. I don't want to push too hard, just work round the key people.

Here he is notably non-specific about what networking involved, appearing to downplay his networking activities by simplifying them to 'just' going to see people and insisting that he does not want to push too hard. This reticence to outline what occurs within these interactions or their outcomes means adopting a discursive contradiction: he is 'just' going to see people and does not want to push 'too hard', yet he also has a clear strategy: working around the key people, letting them know he is looking and keeping in touch. It indicates an understanding that there is a correct and incorrect way to perform these behaviours and that he maintains a subtlety, which is characteristic of British 'gentlemanly' modes of interaction (Augar, 2008).

In a similar way, Linda talks about how she meets people for coffee as part of her networking strategy.

LINDA [SECOND INTERVIEW]: I wouldn't say that. I go in to refresh their memory on who I am, what I've done, remind them why they liked me and when they saw me last, surreptitiously. I've been very casual about it I suppose. But also to bring people up to speed with what I've done since they knew me.

Here again, we see this contradiction manifest in candidates' accounts: Linda describes both strategic and subtle networking: she is 'casual' and surreptitious but has a clear objective about who she networks with and what she aims to achieve in the interaction; again, it is interesting to read this alongside the quote earlier where she refers to herself as becoming a 'CV tart'. This implies that while she might have an overall networking strategy, it is important for her networking interactions to appear 'casual': both to the people she is networking with and to me as the interviewer. She emphasises the need to be surreptitious while reminding her network 'who she is' and why they 'liked' her.

ISABEL (SECOND INTERVIEW): I have to say, and other people have warned me of this, I slightly baulk at the thought of asking, "What are you going to do for me?" That feels very intrusive. Especially if you haven't a long work experience, for someone who you know but not intimately enough to say, "What are you going to do for me?" It's a crowded marketplace and that just doesn't feel comfortable.
SCARLETT: Yeah. It's a difficult conversation [to have].
ISABEL: Exactly. I tend to feel that by virtue of you BEING there, as long as you signal that you are interested in the space, I think any more than that is I don't want to judge others, it just, for me, feels a little uncomfortable.

While candidates talked a lot about the importance of networking, being visible to the right people and indicating that they are looking for roles, it was often unclear from their accounts how this would lead to them being chosen. We can see this dilemma in Isabel's account: when networking is the sole route to roles, you have to be visible, and you have to persuade people to put you forward. For Isabel, this is problematic, and again, we see how she emphasises the need to be subtle: it is uncomfortable to ask people to put her forward because she perhaps does not know them well enough. Because there is little clarity about how to convert visibility into being put forward, the emphasis is placed on 'signalling' that she is interested (again drawing on subtle discourses), and maintaining visibility is the active networking 'practice'. Many interviewees also used this kind of spatial language: visibility means being 'in the space' ('by virtue of you being *there*'), which she feels is a 'crowded marketplace'.

The way that Isabel describes the need to be subtle is also individual-ised: rather than stating why it needs to be subtle, she attributes it to her *feeling uncomfortable* pushing herself forward for board roles because she does not want to be 'intrusive' or pushy. Isabel's statement, 'I don't want to judge others, but' could also be seen as a disclaimer (Gill, 2000): used to prefix something negative before saying something that might be viewed as negative by the interviewer. By stating she doesn't *want* to judge others—and then affirming that she *personally* feels uncomfortable—it could be interpreted that she offers an underlying criticism of those who are 'intrusive' while still presenting herself in a positive light as someone who is not judgemental.

BELINDA [SECOND INTERVIEW]: But I haven't been shameless about it. I'm not good at cold-calling. I'm not good at selling myself, and so I've been trying to be slightly more subtle.

A similar discourse is seen in Belinda's comment, where she describes her networking practices and suggests that she needs to be subtle in how she goes about it. Again, it is interesting that she explains this not by saying it will lead to success but that she *personally* does not want to be 'shame-less'; she states that she is *not good* at selling herself rather than it will be less successful. The notion of being 'shameless' was common in women's narratives and absent from men's and seems to evoke a kind of 'desperate woman' trope: a stereotype that women are more concerned with than men and work harder to avoid.

References that candidates made to being subtle were often implied through the language that they used. It was, therefore, not always clear why the subtlety was necessary (and an explanation was not given in the interviews). Daniel's account, next, is a little different and was one of few that directly mentioned that there could be a penalty for not networking 'correctly'.

DANIEL [SECOND INTERVIEW]: It really is all about your networks (. . .). If you're starting with a blank sheet of paper and no real personal intro-ductions, personal door-opening ability, then I think it's immensely hard task, and if you approach headhunters cold, if you spray your CV around cold, I think you can classically confuse activity with treatment and feel you've been incredibly busy, you've sent hundreds of CVs but actually you've done [nothing]. If anything, you may have hindered your chances because once (.) if you're going to enter the arena you want to do it in the right way.

Daniel's statement draws on the contrasting subtle and strategic net-working discourses: he emphasises the importance of networking to get roles but specifies that this has to be done through recommendations and getting other people to provide personal introductions and to 'open doors' to people who may be able to offer him positions. He similarly emphasises the importance of being subtle in going about these networking practices. He goes even further to suggest that networking in the wrong way (by being too forward) can be *detrimental* to a person's chances of success. The idea that one can network *too* much or too hard suggests that there is a fine balance between being strategic and being subtle and that this is a difficult discourse for candidates to navigate.

The difficulty of navigating the balance between strategic and subtle networking is even more acute in the second and third interviews, as the candidates expressed the difficulties they face maintaining visibility and continuing their networking practices while remaining subtle.

GRACE [SECOND INTERVIEW]: And so I've had a number of conversations with those chairmen following on afterwards, and I think some of them have said to me, "You've got to do this full time if you want to find the right non-exec role. (.) You've got to be absolutely 110% focused on it entirely and keep driving it" (.), and I think they're probably right (.), but there's only so many times you can phone a chairman up of the FTSE 100.
SCARLETT: Yeah, what do you do for those? Thirty, 40 hours a week?
GRACE: Exactly! (.) You know, that's a lot of hours to fill, kind of, you know, phoning the same 100 chairman (.), and it's not even the 100 chairman, because by the time you whittle it down to the ones that you know you're going to add value on and the ones that have got spaces coming up. You know, even across the FTSE 100 and 250, there's probably only 40 boards that you can potentially target.

In this extract, Grace draws heavily on a strategic networking discourse to make sense of the appointment process, describing networking as a full-time job, something that has to be continuously done in order to be successful. However, this highlights the impossibility and contradiction of networking: while it is something that has to be done all the time, there are only a relatively small number of people who sit in positions of power and who can act as gatekeepers to board roles. This narrow access point contributes to candidates' need to target specific individuals and to be highly strategic in how and with whom they network.[1]

GRACE (SECOND INTERVIEW): And so I understand what they're saying, and I understand your networks are important, and I do spend a lot of time focusing on those but (.) you need to just be able to kind of follow those through, I think on, uh, just touch in occasionally to follow through. So I'm kind of thinking that even if we touch base with them once a quarter, it sort of feels like you're already pushing it quite hard (.) and you (.) not appearing, not wanting to appear (.) too desperate.

In this second extract, Grace draws on a discourse of subtle networking; alongside her insistence that she needs to gain visibility and continually work at maintaining it, there is concern that this has to be done in the right way. Grace's response suggests concern that she is appearing 'too desperate' and an insistence that she has to remain subtle and 'just touch in occasionally' with the key individuals. The idea that she might appear 'too desperate' also links to the discourses described earlier, where the implication is that working too hard to contact the people appointing for boards may be detrimental to their chances, giving off the wrong impression and (presumably) leading to failure.

The way that candidates make sense of this networking dilemma is also gendered. While men evoked the importance of being subtle and not being too pushy, women more commonly expressed concern about being seen as 'desperate', discursively portraying a stereotypical trope of the 'desperate woman' (even those who used it positively, such as Linda describing herself as a 'CV tart'). In contrast, the men I spoke to were more likely to describe themselves as being patient and waiting for roles to come to them.

NICHOLAS [THIRD INTERVIEW]: So now I think I'm just being (.) more opportunistic I would say, not systematic. The process I went through in that starting phase was more systematic, but I don't feel I have to do that so much now. I think it's more opportunistic and the network taking over.

Nicholas in particular attributes his change to a more 'opportunistic' way of networking, which he compares to his previous systematic networking (he was our interviewee who aimed for '100 contacts in 100 days'). Instead, now he sees the 'network taking over' and, most importantly, presents this as a reason for him not needing to push as hard with the networks. While for women there is an implication that visibility is something that must be constantly worked on and upheld, men much more commonly described it as if it was something gained at the outset and then maintained through more gentle or subtle networking. Men use patience as an explanation for being subtle rather than a concern with appearing desperate.

IAN [SECOND INTERVIEW]: Things have been ^coming in from time to time^ [from headhunters], and when they didn't come for a while I (.) after a respectable period of time, I'd ring them and say, "Can I come round for a cup of coffee?" But it wasn't very pushy, you know, I wasn't that concerned to move that fast.

Similarly, the way Ian describes his networking foregrounds the need to be subtle and not 'pushy' but also accounts for it by stating that he is not concerned with moving fast. Adopting patience as an explanatory discourse was particularly common in men's accounts and is explored in greater detail in the following chapter; however, here it is specifically used in relation to subtle networking and as a way of explaining Ian's reluctance to push for a role. Again, we see an idea of how individuals might network 'incorrectly', in this case not waiting an acceptable time before re-initiating contact.

The Recommendation

We have seen so far in interviewees' accounts the prevalence of strategic and subtle networking discourses. The contradiction between these perspectives is particularly important when we look at the effects that strategic yet subtle networking has had on how candidates can network and get access to board roles. Another way this strategic yet subtle networking manifested was in candidates feeling that they needed to be recommended, and this was particularly important when networking with headhunters. Headhunters only appear to take on new clients through recommendation, and to get a recommendation, one has to be part of the same network. This supports both strategic and subtle networking: individuals use their connections to strategically gain visibility with a wider network of people by asking their connections to put them in touch with other people; similarly, being recommended is more 'acceptable' and subtle than contacting individuals themselves. In the case of headhunters, it was felt that introductions were necessary in order to be successful.

RAYMOND [SECOND INTERVIEW]: People have been very encouraging and have often (.) offered to introduce me to headhunters, so most of the connections I've had with headhunters have been through my network because it's quite important, I've found with headhunters, to be introduced and not to go in too low.

Raymond here describes the importance of being introduced to headhunters through his network, and this echoes Linda and Gary's statements earlier, both of whom had strong connections to (and/or friendships with) headhunters as a result of their previous careers. Gary describes how he has used his network to introduce him to headhunters but that this is important to ensure that he does not go in 'too low'—i.e. get introduced to a junior headhunter who is seen as having little power (cf. Faulconbridge *et al.*, 2009).

BELINDA [FIRST INTERVIEW]: Well, what I don't know, and this is an uncertainty, is the extent to which there's any value in approaching headhunters directly because it seems like, as Groucho Marx would say,

"You're more attractive when they're looking for you [than when] you're looking for them".

Belinda states that she feels there is little value approaching headhunters directly, instead needing to be approached or recommended, as it conveys their credibility.

BELINDA [SECOND INTERVIEW]: [Headhunters] hold the keys to the fort, they really do. (.) And (.) you know, I've had reasonably good experience with them over time. But I (.) just (.) I don't know (.) you know, they also don't do it on a reverse enquiry basis. It's very (.) I only know one (. . .) who is happy to take what I would call reverse enquiry. So I will often send her women who are looking that I think she will be interested in (. . .). But if anybody is doing that for me, I'm unaware of it; it hasn't come back as feedback. I know of very few people who have approached headhunters directly (.) being in the position of the person looking for the job and had any kind of positive response.

In this extract, we again see how Belinda foregrounds the importance of headhunters, placing them discursively in a position of power as the primary gatekeepers for board roles and the difficulty of getting access to them without recommendations. Although of similar themes, this is discursively different from the accounts of interviewees earlier: Linda and Gary, for instance, do not have the same discomfort with contacting headhunters directly, because they consider or describe them as friends and ex-colleagues rather than as 'cold-calls'. In this way, then, the combination of strategic and subtle discourses emerges in candidates' descriptions of headhunters. This challenges the implicit assumption in much of the research that headhunters are neutral gatekeepers; instead, they are part of the same networks and networking practices.

ISABEL [FIRST INTERVIEW]: I tried to do it through references because I don't think that cold-calling works at all. So I've a friend who is making an introduction to [headhunter] because that is the obvious kind of missing one from my list and precisely because of the (.) slightly position they occupy. I want that to be done by introduction rather than cold-call.

Isabel's description, again, explicitly outlines the importance of being recommended to headhunters as a result of their perceived elite position—here she refers to this as the headhunters' 'slightly' position—their seniority or elite perception; she is referring to one of the largest and most prestigious firms, and this is used to explain why she needs to be introduced to them by a third party. This account draws on a strategic networking discourse too: Isabel needs to ensure that she meets with all of the headhunters, almost like a collection or portfolio rather than a relationship. However, this has to be done in the right way to ensure that they see her as a credible candidate by being introduced by someone—a friend—already in her network who has a pre-existing connection with this headhunter. The introduction, therefore, has a functional advantage, as well as meaning that the headhunter sees her as a credible candidate.

In many cases, the need to be recommended was explicitly stated, and there were accounts of candidates facing difficulty when seeking contact with headhunters without a previous connection.

SCARLETT: So how did that [networking] go?

ISABEL [SECOND INTERVIEW]: I got a range that you would expect, at what was perceived to be a young potential non-exec coming from a no-board background.

SCARLETT: So what sort of things were you getting?

ISABEL: Some, almost without exception, they say, "Oh, it is lucky that the great and the good so-and-so introduced you to us, because otherwise we wouldn't have bothered seeing you", and that is quite disappointing as a candidate; you want to be seen for who you are; you don't want to be seen as a favour to your senior partner. Also, it just really shows, if you haven't got that sponsorship at the top level, I would have thought it is nigh on impossible.

Isabel's use of the word 'sponsorship', which is being supported by someone else who puts his or her reputation on the line (Ibarra *et al.*, 2010), is particularly significant here, as it reiterates the importance of being recommended by other individuals in her network, and she states that this is the *only* route to success. In her account, not having previous board experience (again drawing on the right experience discourse we discussed in the previous chapter) means that the headhunters would not have seen her without the recommendation from her 'sponsor', demonstrating how being recommended can act as a marker of her credibility or calibre, which outweighs the significance of not having the 'right experience'. That she describes the headhunters' response as 'what you would expect' highlights the strength of the right experience discourse: it is a taken for granted, common sense understanding that candidates with no previous board experience will face difficulty due to headhunters' narrow criteria. Isabel also draws on discourses of meritocracy, and its incompatibility with only being seen as a 'favour' to her senior partner—a senior partner at the law firm she works at. This suggests discomfort with the system operating as it does (based on networks and being recommended), as it contradicts notions of meritocracy (being seen for 'who you are'). This disappointment sits alongside her assertion that success will come from networks and an awareness that she has to 'play the game' in order to be appointed. This suggests that (particularly) women in these roles are invested in the notion of merit and wanting to be seen for 'who they are', which is incompatible with the way directors are appointed.

TOM [THIRD INTERVIEW]: So if you've brought in by a headhunter who is standing behind you saying, "We've sought this person out, and this is the reason we sought them out, and, therefore, you should take a look at them", or if you come in as this person who has already done one of those jobs elsewhere, has already been NED or on several boards elsewhere, in which case its incredibly easy to get shortlisted. But starting from scratch, it's impossible.

Tom draws on a similar discourse, this time also stating how the recommendation from the headhunter can work when being put forward for roles. In a similar way to Isabel, he also draws on the right experience discourse to highlight a hypothetical candidate who will find it 'incredibly easy': someone who has the right experience or the right level of sponsorship from someone who can put them forward for roles.

Rather than occupying a separate or distinct space to the wider networks, headhunters were often described in similar terms to their networks and relationships with other directors, treated and referred to as friends and colleagues. This is important to highlight because although it has been discussed in the academic literature on executive search firms (e.g. Beaverstock *et al.*, 2015), policy recommendations on women on boards and corporate governance largely treat the use of search firms as a way of formalising the process (see, for example, Davies, 2011; Financial Reporting Council, 2018; Doldor *et al.*, 2012) or as 'accidental activists' who were a crucial driver towards increasing the representation of women on boards (Doldor *et al.*, 2016). This does not interrogate headhunters' roles in maintaining the status quo or on reproducing the same network dynamics.

The discourses interviewees use to describe their interactions with headhunters suggest that headhunters have and reproduce their own hierarchies within wider networks: certain search firms and individuals are regarded as having access to potential board roles, and these are the primary targets. This is supported by the wider literature on the appointment process, which suggests that headhunters are involved in the majority of board appointment processes in the FTSE 100 and FTSE 250 (Lowe *et al.*, 2016); however, it is important to note that while a company might state that it used a headhunter, this simply means that the search firm manages the appointment process; it does not guarantee that the person appointed was not known to the board already or that the process does not rely on networks.

'New Girl's' Networks

The importance of recommendations also emerged throughout candidates' accounts when they were discussing their networks and networking practices. It was also found in the way that particularly women discussed how they used their networks reciprocally: recommending each other for roles and making introductions for other women. The way that women discussed these networks was particularly interesting: first they justified it in highly pragmatic and practical terms, and, secondly, they frequently framed them in relation to feminist ideals of gender equality: to make up for the disadvantages they face as women, they have to network and form connections with other women.

CATRIN [FIRST INTERVIEW]: And so that was a personal contact, then I don't think I was on the headhunter's original list but then I went on their list after they've spoken to somebody else.

SCARLETT: Okay, and is that someone who you'd worked with before or was it a friend or—?

CATRIN: No, it's someone who I know through the [women on boards] network (.) And we have become friends because we're the two people who are running their non-executive program, so she and I, you know, we do end up being with one another quite a lot, and we are both doing portfolio career, so often if one of us can't do it or doesn't want to do it, we will say, "Have you thought about?" and [each] will recommend the other, as well as other people, of course.

While both men and women noted the importance of being recommended to headhunters as discussed earlier, women's discourses often included an imperative to recommend *other women* and be recommended by them in return. As in Catrin's account, women seeking board roles frequently described relationships they have with other women who are also seeking board roles, and how they work together in their networking practices. This meant recommending each other for roles or introducing each other to headhunters, forming more structured or formal networks and attending similar events.

RACHEL [SECOND INTERVIEW]: I am involved in a diversity-related initiative: I chair a group called [network name], which is about board diversity. As a result of that, someone came to us and said, "We want-" they didn't say a female, but of course, they meant a female, "with finance experience in investment trust". I gave them five names, including my own, and including someone who I knew was the best fit for what they had described, who was the one they chose.

Rachel's account here similarly provides an example of how the formal women's networks function to recommend each other, in this case with the inference that the board or headhunter was looking for a woman with her kind of experience and for which she put a list of women forward. This operates as a formalised version of the need to recommend other women and demonstrates how the incitement to recommend women is an implicit discourse surrounding board appointments.

BELINDA [SECOND INTERVIEW]: So I have put her forward for roles when I've been rung up by the headhunter, and the other thing I did, ^which actually was quite helpful^, is like, I documented my journey, and I keep it updated. So I share this with other people, so when I meet somebody, I give this to them; it's my contacts; it's my learning; it's my tips; it's basically giving forward, being into yoga and all that; this stuff comes back in weird shapes and forms; it completely gets paid back. So, you know, as Margaret [sic] Albright rightly says, "There is a special place in hell for women who don't help women". I completely believe in that, so you just help everyone that you can see.

The Madeline Albright quote, '[t]here is a special place in hell for women who don't help other women' (Albright, 2016), was repeated by a number of the women in the research to emphasise the importance of recommending each other for roles. This suggests a way that certain corporate feminist-sounding 'mottos' become recycled and reproduced in candidates' narratives and could be thought of as being 'made into truth' through their repetition. This in itself of course is not problematic; however, it is notable that if there is a special place in hell for women who do not help other women, this does not give responsibility to the men in the networks (is there a special place in hell for men who do not help women?) and places additional pressure on women who have 'made it' to use their networks or capital to further other women, something that could impact their own positions in the networks too.

GRACE [FIRST INTERVIEW]: I don't know if you've ever heard this really good speech by Christine Lagarde, but I will tell you about it because it's such a good anecdote, it should be on the front of your thesis. She's my heroine; my complete heroine. And she did a speech at my old university. So she tells this story: "When I was at the treasury, one of my jobs was to fill the boards (. . .) so I would send out to all my staff to find some people, and the lists that came back, it was funny, but there were no women on them, almost none. So I made a list of all the women I knew who I thought were qualified for directorships on boards. Every time a man comes up to me and says, 'I'd so love to hire a woman, but we have no qualified women, we could not find a name', I take out my list; I open it and say, 'Have one of mine'. And I recommend all you put together a list, and the next time someone asks you, make sure you have an entire list of qualified women you would be welcome to suggest!" Isn't that great? Anyway, so when I'm putting my list of good people, she [fellow NED] is always on it.

Several women in the research also referenced this speech by Christine Lagarde, the former managing director and chairman of the International Monetary Fund (2011–2019) and president of the European Central Bank from late 2019. Lagarde is a prominent public voice on women in leadership (she also became infamous for stating that if Lehman Brothers had been Lehman Sisters, the crisis might not have happened) to emphasise the importance of recommending each other. Like the quotation from Madeline Albright, these stories became part of candidates' narratives that inform their sense making and how they approach networking. This highlights how candidates draw on corporate feminist-sounding ideas as part of their sense making, mobilising it to emphasise the importance of recommending and supporting other women. It also indicates how such gender knowledge is transmitted at women's events through keynote speeches and reproduced in individual accounts to make sense of their own experiences, particularly in relation to gender.

While both men and women discussed the importance of being recommended as a way to access key individuals, women far more commonly discussed recommending others, something that was notably absent from men's accounts. In contrast to other studies that suggest women may be reluctant to take up the 'women in management' mantle (Mavin, 2006) or engage in female misogyny and negative intra-gender relations (Mavin and Grandy, 2012), women in this research did not suggest a reluctance to promote other women. They did, however, draw on the idea of 'female solidarity' in highly strategic and pragmatic ways, assuming that it would benefit their progression in the long term, much more often than for altruistic or feminist reasons.

SARAH [SECOND INTERVIEW]: I sussed out that, especially with the first headhunter conversation, I realised that they keep calling the same people. And I thought, "Okay, there's very few women that are NEDs, so I am going to network with the women that are NEDs that I know to let them know that I'm looking for-" Now, they can't find me another job (.), but they will remember me, and they will send a, they will let the headhunter know if they're looking for somebody.

This way of networking with each other in highly strategic ways can be interpreted in a number of ways. First, it shows these women having a clear sense of how the system operates (relying as it does on networks and being recommended) and of learning the 'rules of the game' (Kelan and Dunkley Jones, 2010). This can also be seen as finding strategic ways to navigate the informal appointment process and, therefore, another way of 'strategic networking', as discussed earlier in the chapter.

Women's insistence that they recommend each other, as well as being used as a discourse to make sense of their networking practices, has a wider discursive effect in the way that it occludes criticism of the process relying on networks.

TINA [SECOND INTERVIEW]: It demonstrates how, you know, it is all about networks. But when you are [female] there isn't the Old Boys' network to claw at. And I'm not knocking it because, frankly, I do the same now with women. I will introduce whenever I can; I will help other women. So I'm going to be doing the same as they [the men] do, it's just that our networks are in their infancy compared to theirs.

Women often mentioned the Old Boys' networks when describing why they recommended other women for roles; however, this was often presented in a rational and uncritical way that sees building 'New Girl's' networks' as a necessary way of tackling men's homophily and the historical problem of Old Boys' networks. In Tina's account here, we see how this is described fairly uncritically, where the networks are a taken-for-granted part of the process, and their suggestions for how to tackle the lack of women is to use their own networks to put women forward.

SARAH [SECOND INTERVIEW]: So you know that is exactly what the chaps do [recommending each other], and so I am just as happy to do it. I'm not criticising them for doing it; it's just that they don't realise they do it; they just think they are being terribly helpful and unselfish. There's no woman within that network; therefore, they are unconsciously never helping women, and they are always helping men. It's just that the numbers game is such that there are, you know, few men who are going to rush out and help the women.

Sarah uses a similar discursive repertoire to explain why she recommends other women for roles but expands further to describe men's tendency to recommend each other; the inference is that women need to emulate men in order to be successful rather than challenging the process and how it operates. In her account, it is taken for granted that men recommend each other unconsciously, and that this is a result of a historical gender imbalance rather than deliberately excluding women. This extract contains a contradictory discursive device in the sense that Sarah implies that while her networking is done deliberately, men's homophily or tendency to help other men is neither conscious nor deliberate. She, therefore, offers an explanation that is almost entirely devoid of critique or discussion of power imbalances and instead is just something women will have to work around by helping each other.

Avoiding the 'Handbag Society'

We saw in the previous section how, particularly women, describe the importance of recommending each other, putting other women forward for roles and, in some cases, forming all-women networks of aspiring directors as a way to address the historic imbalance between their networks and men's networks. This was often described as a way of learning the 'rules of the game': navigating an appointment process reliant on networks and that favours those candidates who have stronger connections with current directors.

Somewhat contradictorily, we also found that women spoke very critically of all-women networks and events they had attended.

ALEXANDRA [SECOND INTERVIEW]: So, there is a new trend, which is in my view highly objectionable because it's a waste of time = and that it is when headhunters say, "Oh, I'm going to organise the networking event for all these women who want to be NEDs". Right so they organise a networking event and everyone is a woman who wants to be a NED, and that's it. There is no one there with a job or no one there with any insight. You're there, and you're networking with each other, and they feel good about themselves, and you're just like [exhales].

Alexandra's account of women's networking events was typical of women's accounts throughout the research: while informal networking is described as necessary or unavoidable, formal networking is 'objectionable' or a 'waste of time'. Her account here describes a particular kind of networking that occurs within a quasi-public space: a women-on-boards networking event, often organised by headhunters or large professional services firms to engender connections between women and between aspiring directors and potential gatekeepers. This account is in stark contrast to the discourses presented in the previous section where we saw how women speak positively about the potential of women's networks; instead, here these formalised events are criticised, largely because they do not lead to connections with the right people. This again highlights the primacy of the strategic networking discourse, as it demonstrates how candidates frequently judge the success of networking events by the likelihood of success and the seniority of the attendees: networking is judged purely on whether it is likely to lead to forming more connections rather than something done socially, casually or over a long period of time (as was evident in men's discourses). Women seemed to have highly strategic perspectives of their networking to criticise these spaces, and this is in contrast to the literature that argues that men's networks are more instrumental and readily used for self-promotion and increasing their own visibility (Forret and Dougherty,

2001; Ibarra, 1992, 1993) or that women's affective connection with their friends prevents them from using workplace friends in an instrumental way (Mavin *et al.*, 2012, 2013)

SARAH [FIRST INTERVIEW]: Then I find (. . .,) I have to be honest with you, there are very few of these women's organisations which are anything more than talking shops. (.) So I've been very limited in how much attendance [sic].

In the extract, Sarah is also highly critical of 'women's' (networking) events, here describing them as a 'talk[ing] shop'—i.e. someplace where unproductive talking occurs but that does not offer practical support, action or increase her likelihood of being appointed. It being a 'women's organisation' (and her emphasising it being women) describes the network in similar ways to the wider literature: women's networks are seen as unproductive and not focused on action. While the wider literature suggests that women can find support in such networks, this also suggests that in the case of women at very senior levels, the emotional or affective aspect is also not seen as useful. This could be seen as a way for these women to 'do gender differently': they emphasise their professional identities and deliberately move away from 'unproductive and feminine sociality' (Benschop, 2009: p. 233) by emphasising the instrumental function of their networks.

TINA [SECOND INTERVIEW]: Far and away, the majority of the people in that room were women, and for me, you know, that is not the best environment. The men are not coming to something like this; they don't need to, and the key individuals who are making decisions about the next people on their board or around their tables are not here. (. . .) It is not worth just debating and discussing eternally because the reality is that the decision makers are men.

Tina similarly draws on the strategic networking discourse to describe all-female networks, noting that they are not a valuable use of her time because they are talk based and not attended by people who may be able to put her onto boards. It is also notable that men were described as not 'needing' to attend these networking events; it is taken for granted that men will already have access to the right networks and, therefore, do not need to attend these specific events, emphasising again the problems associated with women-only spaces.

TINA [THIRD INTERVIEW]: I am meeting some very nice and interesting people and having nice conversations, but so what? (.) It just felt like everyone was trying, and it was a great idea, and this was a nice networking event, and it was free, so you kind of go, "Okay, well it makes a bit more sense". But it was really interesting just standing back and saying, "Okay, so who is here?" And if you had known who was here beforehand, would you think it was the right thing to go to?

In Tina's third interview, she draws on similar discourses (as in her second interview) to criticise the women-only networking spaces as a waste of her time that did not introduce her to high-profile individuals, again suggesting that the value of the events is measured in highly strategic and targeted terms. This discourse is also gendered, placing the sociality and 'niceness' in opposition to a more tangible use of actively gaining useful connections.

SCARLETT: So do you feel like the more formal networking is not as useful?
TINA [THIRD INTERVIEW]: Certainly, events like that I don't think are particularly useful. I think the events that are quite targeted around something specific, like if you are debating a particular issue, then it is useful to get people together to discuss that, and if you have a balanced, a sort of gender balance, ethnicity, ethnically balanced group of people, I think you will get something more out of it. But I think if it's the Handbag Society, there is no point in it. If I am speaking at an event, now I will not speak at a women-only event.

Here again Tina criticises the formal networking events for not being useful in gaining the right connections and again explicitly states that the problem is the lack of diversity. She emphasises its superficiality, particularly when she goes on to describe a hypothetical 'useful' event that has a clear objective or function. Referring to women's networks pejoratively as 'handbag' societies is an extreme use of the gendered discourse, drawing a connection between superficial and highly feminised spaces, placing femininity in opposition to usefulness and using femininity as a way to denote her disdain.

LINDA [SECOND INTERVIEW]: I hate this rubber chicken circuit[2] stuff, which I think of as going along to a breakfast with 12 other women, all of whom are quite shamelessly trying to get the chairman's attention by saying anything and everything. And I'm sitting there thinking, 'What a bloody waste of time this is'.

As with the way women adopted the subtle networking discourse, Linda refers to shame and 'shamelessness' in regard to women who network in an incorrect or unsubtle way—for example, those who are trying too hard to get the attention of the chairman [sic] at the event. This can be seen as a form of negative intra-gender relations (Mavin and Grandy, 2016a, 2016b) through being critical of other women, using gendered language to do so, and implicitly drawing on ideas of certain women being inappropriate, unsubtle or shameless. We also see how the strategic networking discourse is deployed to criticise based on the assertion that the events are a 'waste of time'.

It is worth bearing in mind in relation to Linda's description that the activities she describes—women trying to be visible to chairs—is a necessary function of networking for non-executive roles; their networking practices require them to get the attention of chairs in some way or another. Her criticism suggests, therefore, that there is a 'correct' way to get this attention—one involving subtlety and authenticity—rather than simply attending events for the sake of it or doing 'anything and everything' to get the chair's attention.

LINDA [THIRD INTERVIEW]: I found it interesting, only because of the opportunity to that there were so many chairmen in the room. Again, I found it frustrating, this gaggle of people who just want to sit there and either say nothing or say lots. Some are very helpful, it was there I met [female NED], and she was very impressive, and you had the opportunity for a proper conversation. But, no, I have to confess, I have my, this is one of my flat sides, I just cannot be asked to do all of this self-promotion business in front of 16 million others. It's just shameless prostitution as far as I'm concerned.

In Linda's third interview, she uses similar discourses to criticise women's networking events, again using highly gendered language to describe women who did not network subtly and referring to it this time even more strongly as 'shameless prostitution'. The discursive creation of two opposing kinds of people who are networking incorrectly (people who 'want to sit there and either say nothing or say lots') is particularly interesting, as it clearly highlights the double-bind between being strategic and active in networking and needing to be subtle and not say 'too much'. Again, as discussed earlier, Linda notes that meeting one key ('impressive') person was a positive outcome of the event, but this is contrasted with the other women who were not useful connections for her.

Measuring success according to the seniority, impressiveness or calibre of the individuals attending an event was found in many interviewees' accounts, highlighting how directors draw on notions of elite status to describe their networking. When events are attended by individuals who the candidate perceives as being of a lower calibre to them, they often described it as a waste of time, such as in Danielle's account, which follows, when discussing re-attending an annual NED training event:

DANIELLE [THIRD INTERVIEW]: I also have to say that I felt that the last time I went to the [networking event] that the quality and the calibre and the seniority of the women that were attending was a lot lower. They're sending people on it who are not ready to sit on boards.

And so for the women that are there and have had those experiences, I personally thought: "I'm not going to do this again", because I don't feel that the calibre of the people you are putting on it is sufficiently high for me to be regarded in the same group. They haven't had, they haven't had board experience.

As well as the gendering of the spaces and criticism due to their women-only quality, women often criticised these spaces due to the low calibre of candidates attending them and a perception that they themselves are therefore 'too' senior or well connected for their attendance to be useful. Notably, this also relates to the importance of previous board experience, which is seen as a key factor in candidates being of high enough calibre to join boards; as Danielle has previous board experience, she feels she is of a higher calibre than the other women there.

KAREN [SECOND INTERVIEW]: [They're only useful] if you see the senior person you see a lot of the problems with a lot of the 'women's initiatives', as I call them, is that they've been set up by one person who is typically very good. If you end up speaking to that person, you probably have a good dialogue. If you don't, you end up with a bunch of people who generally have fewer contacts in the market than you do. I mean, most of the time, I have to be honest and say, most of the time when I've gone along to talk to these women's network things, by the time I get to telling them who I've already talked to, they are sitting there thinking, "My God, where do I go from here?"

Karen adopts a very similar narrative to Danielle and once again evokes the strategic networking discourse to account for why women-on-boards networking events are not helpful for her. Karen's account also connects to the networking discourses described earlier in that she makes reference to the key gatekeepers (in this case a senior headhunter seen as a valuable connection) but is critical of other people's ability to help her get roles. This suggests that the one-on-one networking (often favoured by men in their networking practices) is seen as the most valuable kind of networking and that this group networking is 'useless' by comparison.

Men in this research talked very little about attending formal events as part of their networking (see also Brown *et al.*, 2015); rather, men's networking was nearly always described in terms of one-on-one interactions with individuals who could give them access to boards or in terms of gaining visibility. The only exception was that two of the men interviewed had completed the Financial Times NED diploma, a training course (which several of the women had taken too) that purports to prepare candidates for being an effective NED, with some inference that it can lead to being appointed. Those who had completed this gave fairly negative feedback for similar reasons to the criticisms of women's networks: it did not lead to them being put forward for roles.

SCARLETT: Would you recommend it [training course] to a friend? Would you recommend it to someone in your position who is doing a similar [thing]?

ANTHONY [FIRST INTERVIEW]: It depends why they want to do it I think. My experience so far is that it makes no difference whatsoever to your employability. That the FT talk a good game about, you know, that you would be better educated *et cetera, et cetera*; [but] the head-hunters couldn't care less.

Anthony's account here adopts the strategic networking discourse even more strongly than in the women's accounts, measuring the success of the training course through its capability of getting him a board role, as the headhunters do not recognise it as valuable experience. This again reiterates the role that headhunters have in defining the ideal board member (as discussed in the previous chapter) and as gatekeepers to roles; his negative feedback is centred on what the headhunters perceive as being valuable.

The only other director-specific event that men discussed was a sector-specific network related to getting lawyers onto boards. When those men who had attended discussed it, it was often couched in the 'right experience' discourse described earlier, as it focused on getting visibility (in a broad sense) for lawyers and demonstrating that lawyers can make a valuable contribution; it was less frequently described as a networking opportunity for individual attendees. One of the women lawyers in the research also discussed this network, as she had been invited to join it, and her account highlighted the potential gendered ghettoising that can occur in director networks.

DANIELLE [THIRD INTERVIEW]: Just to demonstrate how the Old Boys' network is alive and kicking, our HR director here, who I've got a lot of time for, he said to me, "Do you want to go on this programme that [organisation] are running?" Because their model works whereby they get [organisations] to pay them a nominated amount, and they can send a number of [people] on this programme to help them get NED positions. And that's great, but, you know, I know if I went out and said, "Can I have some money for this great programme to help women?" I would have been BEGGING. I mean it's good, and you do support it, but he sent me details, sort of [saying], "These guys are mates of mine; they've set this up. Would you go on it with a few other people because I need to put some people on it?" So I go to it and it's for, you know, ex-public school; Oxbridge. And I just thought, "I can't". And they are trying to establish a service to help these non-execs, and I'm thinking, "Fine if you're like them, the Old Boys, you will enjoy it". But if you're a woman, would that be of any interest to you? Zippo. So, you know, so that exists, so when I had my male mates say, "Oh, how do you get non-execs?" I would recommend them, but I won't recommend women because I just know they won't like it, you know?

Daniella's was one of few accounts that saw a woman discussing an event in negative terms because it was majority men, and she felt that made it an exclusionary environment for women. Rather than criticising it for being helpful to her networking (the most common critique of women's networks), she points out that the network being solely made up of individuals from a traditional Old Boys' network made it most applicable or enjoyable for individuals who were also like them. This presents a contradiction, where the spaces are seen as problematic and, perhaps, as enviable because they are majority male but also as places that women would not enjoy. Taken with the overall criticisms of the women's networks, this also suggests that the single-gender networks are both ghettoised and exclusionary. The relative lack of networks that are made up of both men and women is a problem for the formation of directors' networks and the potential for change.

All of the women in the research had attended at least one event or were members of a women's network focused on non-executive directors. Despite their view that it was important for women to recommend each other for roles and to form 'New Girl's' networks as a way to get roles and address the (perceived) weaknesses of their networks, they also often described these official women's networks in negative terms. To make sense of women's networking events, they draw on both the strategic networking and subtle networking discourses, criticising the events for not providing them with strategic networking opportunities (and thus being a waste of time) and using the subtle networking discourse to describe (most often critically) the networking behaviours within these women-only spaces.

Women-on-boards networking, therefore, presents a dilemma or double-bind for women seeking non-executive roles: they feel that they have to disassociate themselves, both physically and discursively, from other women in the space, while also relying on other women for recommendations and advocating this process. Over the course of the research, many of the women addressed this double-bind by rejecting women-only spaces and networks and ceasing to attend them as part of their networking practices. This emerged commonly in the second or third interviews when they discussed how their networking practices had changed since the beginning of their search.

This active avoidance of women's spaces and women's networks is reminiscent of other research into women's networks, where many describe their reluctance to join due to the perception that they are highly feminised spaces involved in 'male-bashing and recipe exchanging' (Bierema, 2005: p. 214) that will not help them with career progression. In terms of their networking practices, many of the candidates had started out at the beginning of the research attending many of these events, but over the course of their search, they had decided to stop attending, commonly citing the lack of useful contacts they meet as a reason for them no longer attending the events.

Conclusion

This chapter has explored how aspiring directors network to gain non-executive board roles and the discourses they use to make sense of their networking practices. As was noted in the women-on-boards literature, we found that all interviewees prioritised networking in their search for a board role: networking is tacitly understood as the primary (or only) way to be appointed onto a board, and it is a taken-for-granted part of aspiring directors' searches. Candidates' accounts outline how they aim to gain visibility with as many non-executive directors, chairs and headhunters as they can and to let them know that they are seeking board roles through their networking practices.

To make sense of their networking, candidates draw on two primary sense-making discourses. The first we call *strategic networking*: where they describe how they adopt rigorous, deliberate and often highly formal networking strategies to target as many individuals as they can with the aim of gaining visibility. The second discourse is *subtle networking*, which draws on a contrasting discourse of needing to be subtle in their networking practices; they describe how they must not 'push too hard' on boards or headhunters to appoint them, as this is presumed to be detrimental to their success.

The discourses that candidates draw on to describe their networking practices present a highly rational and strategic view of relationships and suggest a kind of commodification of relationships where the aim of networking is to collect or form as many relationships as possible. By listing their connections with headhunters, maintaining spreadsheets of who they have contacted most recently and how to access other people and treating their networking as 'going to see people' (simultaneously seeing anyone they can, while also being targeted and choosy), the way they describe the practice of networking reduces relationships to their strategic function: gaining visibility. This discourse, therefore, challenges the notion that women in particular have strong, affective relationships at work and are less likely to have strategic ones (cf. Mavin and Grandy, 2012); rather, both men and women seeking board roles describe these connections in highly strategic terms. Relationships that cannot provide connections to relevant others or lead to the potential of being appointed are described in highly negative terms; this also emerges in how women describe women's official networks and the notion that connections or events (which do not lead to success) can be a 'waste of time'.

One way of explaining the existence of a subtle networking discourse is to place non-executive directors within a wider class structure and of these discourses as a way to establish or uphold elite identity and part of elite class culture (Savage and Williams, 2008; Savage *et al.*, 2013). Alvesson and Robertson argue that 'elite' identity is different from many other kinds of identity, insomuch as to directly identify with it is to 'imply pretentiousness' (Alvesson and Robertson, 2006: p. 200). Instead, 'cultural or symbolic meanings are implicit and indirectly hinted at' (ibid.). This could underpin candidates' accounts as to how and why they need to network subtly: it is important that they are not too direct or pushy, as members of the elite do not make their elite status known. In this sense, their reluctance to identify themselves as searching for roles or as pushing 'too hard' for success is both reflective of social norms surrounding their networking and the population they identify with. Not wanting to appear pushy is, therefore, a function of elite identity that maintains elite closure.

We also found that interviewees' placed a great deal of importance on being recommended to key individuals as part of their networking. Headhunters in particular are seen as being difficult to approach 'cold' or without an introduction, and there is a perception that search firms will only be interested in candidates who are introduced by someone they already know. This is a barrier to newer candidates who are not already connected to directors, as it makes it difficult for them to contact headhunters out of the blue. Maintaining a barrier to entry is, as noted in the wider literature on executive search firms, part of the professionalisation of their industry: maintaining a high barrier to entry is in their best interest if they are to maintain the notion that they have an exclusive and select range of potential candidates (Beaverstock *et al.*, 2015; Wirz, 2014). Aspiring directors also describe this as a taken-for-granted part of the appointment process, and, therefore, the incitement to recommend each other and seek out recommendations or introductions to headhunters is part of their networking.

The importance of being recommended also contributes to our understanding of how women and men in senior roles rely on sponsors (Ibarra *et al.*, 2010) for their success. Those candidates with sponsors—people prepared to introduce them to key individuals, advocate their ability and recommend them for roles—described the process in more positive terms. Relying on recommendations can place women at a disadvantage because they are less likely to have key advocates or sponsors in senior roles (ibid.); however, these findings also demonstrate that, in the case of directors, sponsors can be individuals who are not necessarily more 'senior'. Candidates were often 'sponsored' by people who were not necessarily more senior than them but better connected to gatekeepers. This also demonstrates the complexity of these networks and the difficulties individuals face if they are not already connected to them. Being recommended for a role also acts as a bridge between needing to be both strategic and subtle in networking practices: being recommended by someone else allows them to be targeted and strategic while remaining subtle. When recommending others, candidates did not express the same concerns with being too pushy, suggesting an interesting inconsistency whereby candidates can push others forward but cannot push *themselves* forward.

We also find that reliance on recommendations and sponsors is gendered in how it is embedded in candidates' discourses. While most candidates (both men and women) discussed the dilemma of needing to be introduced and recommended for roles, particularly when negotiating connections with headhunters, women far more commonly advocated the importance of also *recommending other women* as a way to tackle the historical Old Boys' networks. While men may have recommended each other for roles, it was notably absent in their accounts. While this may represent reality—perhaps women do more commonly recommend others than men—it also reflects women's desire to emphasise these networking practices in the interview, forming part of the self-identity that they wish to portray. Given these references, and most notably the assertion that there is a 'special place in hell for women who do not help other women', this may suggest that the imperative to help other women is part of senior women's self-identity, perhaps to avoid any claim that they are 'Queen Bees' or 'pulling the ladder up' (Mavin and Grandy, 2012) and is a strategic necessity to tackle men's networks.

The importance of networking and recommending other candidates also manifests in women's formal networks. Despite women holding strong views that it was important for women to recommend each other for roles and to form 'New Girl's' networks, official women's networks were described in strongly negative terms, as has been observed in wider research (Bierema, 2005; Kelan, 2010). Overall, there is a problematic contradiction in women's networking accounts. They describe an imperative to network with other women and a need to subvert men's networks, the importance of being recommended and a pseudo-feminist imperative to help other women while simultaneously voicing dissatisfaction with women-only networks. Unlike wider research into women's networks, these networks are described as being used for emotional or affective support; rather, they are criticised because the key powerbrokers in board appointments are most commonly men, and, therefore, formal networking with other women will not help them to get roles.

The way that women describe women's networks can also be seen as part of their gendered, elite sense making, where in the process of discursively criticising the women's networks, they also emphasise their own elite status and use gendered language to speak pejoratively about other women. This discursive combination highlights the importance of understanding women seeking board roles as occupying a unique space as gendered members of an elite (or members of a gendered elite). This is done through reference to both subtle and strategic networking discourses: they speak positively about networking events that result in their being able to gain connections with the right people (strategic networking success) and negatively about women who do not network in the right way (those who do not adopt subtle networking), who are described, amongst other things, as 'shameless'. They also use gendered language to critique the events themselves, which are seen as being primarily focused on talk rather than action.

Notes

1. In additional survey work conducted for this research project (Brown *et al.*, 2015), it was found that women far more so than men were seeking FTSE 350 roles, while men were more likely to approach AIM-listed and private companies. One of the explanations we offered for this was that the focus on getting women onto the FTSE 100 from the Davies Review (Davies, 2011) was driving women's behaviour; they targeted companies that they knew needed to get women. This was one of the successes of the Davies Review in that it encouraged women who perhaps would not have sought roles to see themselves as viable candidates and to go for those roles. The concern we raised, however, is that women targeting these companies meant that they were often not looking at the much wider range of companies that might need non-executives and, therefore, limiting their access to roles.
2. The phrase 'rubber chicken circuit' refers to the rubbery texture of reheated chicken that is served at official functions that political candidates have to attend to garner support.

5 Leaning In and Sitting Back

So far, we have explored how aspiring directors seeking board roles go through the board appointment process and how notions of the ideal board member make the board appointment process impervious to critique. We also explored candidates' reliance on networking and visibility. This has shown how men's and women's networking practices are gendered, with women often ghettoised into women's networks that do not allow them access to key powerbrokers as easily as men. We also saw how gendered expectations result in women having highly targeted and active networking strategies, while men's are more passive. These two aspects are important, as they expand our understanding of the extant research on women on boards, which, as we showed in Chapter 2, focuses on human capital and social capital explanations for women's absence and uses static or quantitative analyses. To build on our understanding, we now zoom out even further to look at how candidates make sense of the process overall and how they account for their successes and failures. This reveals how their discourses are gendered and the wider macro discursive effects of these discourses.

This research involved interviewing men and women several times over the course of three years, during which time many of our interviewees gained board roles and several did not. The longitudinal focus allowed us to talk to them about their successes and failures and how they accounted for them. In making sense of their successes and failures, we found that women draw on neoliberal discourses to make sense of the board appointment process, emphasising the work they have to put into networking, interacting with headhunters and learning how to 'play the game'. Women also accounted for their success as a result of their overcoming internal barriers, such as lack of confidence, or external barriers, such as lack of networked support and being active in their networking practices. They also draw on these discourses to account for their difficulty in getting roles, often implying that it was their inability to overcome these barriers that prevented them from succeeding. This internalisation means that the only solution is to work harder, as there is no external issue to account for their failure.

In contrast, men frequently presented their success as something that came (or will come) with little effort on their part and often as a result of their ability to be patient, choosy and wait for the 'right' role to come to them, what we call a 'sit back' discourse. Similarly, they present failure (at least in terms of not getting a NED role) as resulting either from their decision to be choosy or as a result of the focus on getting women onto boards. Often, men perceived there to be an advantage for women, which meant they had to be patient while boards address diversity by including more women. This affords them a way of explaining both their successes and failures in such a way that they uphold their self-presentation as persons who are or will be successful, and the only thing that needs to change is the presumed influx of women.

The Female Hero

When we asked women to reflect more broadly on the appointment process and their experiences, we found repeated use of neoliberal and individualised rhetoric, which we make sense of here as representing neoliberal and/or corporate feminist discourses (Fraser, 2009, 2013; Gill and Orgad, 2016; McRobbie, 2009, 2013; Roberts, 2015; Rottenberg, 2014, 2018). Academics have theorised this as a particular kind of feminism that adopts an awareness of and challenge to gender inequality and one that is stripped of its moral, political and collective agenda. While historic feminist movements have centred on making gender inequality visible and advocating for women's rights and/or gender equality, a neoliberal feminist subject criticises social, cultural and economic forces that drive gender inequality but advocates for an internalised, self-realised, proactive subjectivity to tackle it (Rottenberg, 2014). This is epitomised in corporate feminist texts, notably Sheryl Sandberg's *Lean In* (Sandberg, 2013), a self-proclaimed feminist manifesto that argues for women's advancement in the workplace and publicly advocates feminist values through women putting themselves forward or leaning in. Analysing this biography alongside others, the figure that emerges through the accounts is that of a female hero who has the confidence, control and courage to avoid any gendered barriers that she encounters (Adamson and Kelan, 2019).

The language of a neoliberal feminist subject was evident throughout women's accounts of their success and failure in gaining board roles over the course of the research. Women who were successful in gaining board roles over the course of the research often attributed their success, either explicitly or implicitly, to their hard work:

LINDA [THIRD INTERVIEW]: I just think, looking back, now my husband has just been amazed. I left [previous company]; I didn't have anything lined up. And he's blown away by the fact that I, basically I've sorted myself out. He turned to me the other day and said, "You've really taken this on as a campaign, haven't you?" And I said, it wasn't. It didn't feel like it, but I suppose when you look back on it, it's you just know what you've gotta do. You've gotta get out there, and you've gotta do stuff that goes against the grain, but, you know, at the end, it's okay; it will pay off.

In looking back at her search for board roles and her subsequent success, Linda uses a narrative that emphasises her hard work and 'campaign' of networking, which she implies has led to her gaining a board role. Her narrative is starkly neoliberal and individualised and presents her as a kind of neoliberal hero: starting with nothing when she retired ('I didn't have anything lined up'), taking on a 'campaign' of networking and pushing herself forward, resulting in success. It is notable that even within this narrative, she emphasises her discomfort with needing to network (doing 'stuff that goes against the grain') but with the overall insistence that it 'will pay off'. This ties to the findings we discussed in Chapter 4, where networking is treated as a 'necessary evil' that aspirant directors have to go through in order to be successful but emphasises how hard she worked to get the role.

She, like many of the women who were successful in gaining a role during the period of the research, is able to account for the networking retrospectively as something that was 'worth doing'. This becomes a rationalisation or acceptance of the system as it is because she is able to navigate it.

ALEXANDRA [SECOND INTERVIEW]: I'm sure the reason why I got put on the list was because I = I went to a cocktail party hosted by that headhunter. And it was a day where I was in Manchester for a board meeting that started at nine in Manchester, so you have to get up at the crack of SPARROWS in the morning to take the train to Manchester. Audit Committee Meeting. Board meetings. Some politics at the end. Some issue with the trains, eventually you get back to London. You really feel like a cocktail party, don't you? You know, make-up since five in the morning, but I just hold my backside in the air and did it = and it just goes to show like you've got to do these things. But if I was listening to my body, I wouldn't have gone there, you know what I mean?

Like Linda, Alexandra attributes her success to hard work and perseverance and adopts a similar heroic narrative, albeit with a gendered twist: where she battled against her discomfort (in this case, the needs of her own body) to go to a networking event, attributing her success to her active networking practices and ability to overcome her physical needs in order to do so. Her reference to having worn 'make-up since five in the morning' adds an additional gendered element to the sense making: wearing make-up is a taken-for-granted and necessary part of her work, a kind of aesthetic labour required for women but not men, while wearing it all day contributes to the overall description of her physical discomfort and the labour required to attend the networking event.

Like Linda, Alexandra's narrative fluctuates between different temporal perspectives by looking back at her networking practices and then being able to attribute her success to them. This discursive process allows her to translate individual success into a wider imperative; because it is what she did and it led to success, it becomes what '*you* have to do (. . .) *you've* got to get out there'. '*You've* got to do these things', drawing strongly on, and reproducing, neoliberal discourses. This discursive shift from an individual's hard work leading to success being extrapolated out to a wider perception on what leads to success, reiterates the importance of attending networking events as a strategy to get roles, despite this being in contradiction to women's description of the networking events, which presented them as being a 'waste of time'. This may suggest, then, that headhunters and networking events are regarded (especially by women) as resources they can and must access as part of their (net)work rather than as something that will actively help them to get roles. This again draws on a neoliberal, individualised discourse to describe elements of the process and her success, which she is able to adopt because of the benefit of hindsight.

Similarly, Laura was appointed to a board during the research period and described the process overall and what she saw as leading to success.

LAURA [THIRD INTERVIEW]: It's a bit like, when you look back, I look back at the last 12 months. It's a bit like ANYTHING else. Getting a job, be it your first job, your second your third job, whatever. It's a little bit about self-promotion; it's a little bit about how you come across in interview; it's a BIT about having the right skills, and then there's a bit of luck. And if you acknowledge that and say "Okay, what does it take for me to do, to get to 'X' and work it out?" A bit like, "Well, what's it going to take for me to get a good job interview?" It's no different! It's just not the SAME. But if you think somebody's going to do you a favour? Forget it. It's far more a case of word of mouth that your CV alone will vouch for. But, you know, once you've worked it out and prepared to put a little leg work in and be a little shameless in pulling your skirt up on the street corner. It's actually- and it's the same for men.

Laura also adopts a neoliberal and individualised discourse to explain the process and how she was able to navigate it successfully. She describes many aspects of the process that contribute to her success: self-promotion, interviewing well, a 'BIT about having the right skills, and a bit of luck'.

That she emphasises a 'bit' appears to reduce her skills in comparison to other aspects that she mentions, and this is echoed later when she asserts that it is 'more word of mouth that the CV will vouch for', reiterating that having the right experience is less important than other aspects. The notion of learning how to play the rules of the game also has the discursive effect of placing the impetus for success on the individual who is responsible for putting the effort in.

That she relates non-exec search to 'any kind' of job is also notable. Later in the interview, she discusses this in relation to her son, who is looking for a job after university, and she notes several similarities between her experience and his. This has the discursive effect of placing a normative framework over the appointment process by drawing on a wider neoliberal discourse—one where no one can expect anyone to 'do it for you' at any level of employment. This does not allow discursive space for challenging the process, as, again, it iterates that it is the same at all levels, even for young men at lower levels of employment. This also points to the tension between 'expecting someone to do you a favour' and it being word of mouth: the word of mouth aspect of the appointment process means, by its very nature, getting someone to 'help'. She reiterates this contradiction further by emphasising how, once you know it's all about word of mouth and recommendations, you then have to put the work in. In her account, (female) candidates need to learn how to play the game, and once they have worked out the rules, the rest is 'just' hard work.

Laura's description of playing the game as 'being shameless in pulling your skirt up on a street corner' uses highly gendered language that likens the work needed for the process to sex work, with a fairly derogatory tone, suggesting a kind of abject femininity. It should also be pointed out that Linda was, in an earlier chapter, talking negatively about women who were 'shameless' in their networking: those whom she did not see as being senior enough to get roles on boards but who were pushing themselves forward. It is interesting then that she uses the word 'shameless' here to describe her own networking practices. This might be an attempt to claim she was being shameless in the 'right' way: because she networked (shamelessly) with people who were able to appoint her, she is different than those women who are doing it shamelessly and failing. On the other hand, it may be a way to describe her realisation that because the system operates in a certain way, the *only* way to navigate it is to behave in a way that she sees as unacceptable or shameless, again presenting networking as a 'necessary evil'. She then states that it is the same for men, which is a curious statement to follow such a gendered phrased, but this has the effect of pre-empting criticism that I might raise and normalising the process: men have to do the same, so it is a 'fair' system. This is also interesting given that our findings suggest that men do not see the networking in the same way; it is literally *not* the same for men. This results in the insistence that the process is gender neutral, even when using highly gendered discourses to describe it.

Working (Within) the System

Another area in which we found women making reference to how hard they worked for success is when describing how they learned to 'play the game', particularly in relation to their relationships with headhunters. Charlotte, next, talked in both her first and second interviews about needing to make sure that the headhunter knows what kind of roles she wants and ensuring that, should she be put forward, there was no doubt that she would say yes.

CHARLOTTE [FIRST INTERVIEW]: The headhunter is a sales person, right? Frankly, they're not your friend; they're not your career advisor; they don't care; they just want the sale. So saying, "Back me because I'll say, yes; if you give me the job, I'll say yes, and you can get your fee". "Yes, I'll say yes to this one". Reassure the headhunter, don't say = "Well, I'm not sure because he had stripes, and I prefer whatever". You can't say that to the headhunter because the headhunter is like, "Crumbs, she may not say yes; I need to get another one. I'd better talk the other one up to the client", but if you say, "I'll say yes; I'll say yes; I'll say yes", she will talk you up to the client.

The interactional work that Charlotte describes needing to put in with the headhunter is remarkable and treats headhunters' decision making as something she needs to work on to make sure that they put her forward for a role. This portrays the headhunter as powerful in the space, but she also takes responsibility for pushing herself forward and doing the work required to be successful. The way she describes this interaction allows her to take credit for her success: in this account, even the headhunter thinking that she was the right candidate and putting her forward for a role is attributed instead to her own persistence and the 'work' she put in to persuade him or her. One the other hand, it also means taking responsibility for her failure: rather than the headhunter being blamed for not putting her forward, she sees it as her responsibility to make sure the headhunter knows she wants the role.

She picks up this same narrative in her second interview:

CHARLOTTE [SECOND INTERVIEW]: Well, at the moment the headhunter— it's still the racehorse of the headhunters, so it's very important that the headhunter knows that you're going to say yes because they're thinking, "Am I going to get my commission?" And, of course, they're only going to get their commission if you're going to say, "Yes". If you say, "Well I'm not quite sure", they're like, "Oh shit", you know: "Let's make sure that the other one is the racehorse that I'll back".

Charlotte adopts the same discourse to explain the process with remarkable consistency, given the interviews were six months apart. There is a 'knowingness' and pragmatism to her narrative, an acknowledgement of bias or problems in the system and how she navigates it. Rather than criticising the process writ large, she uses it as a discursive tool to portray herself as someone who is able to work around it.

CHARLOTTE [THIRD INTERVIEW]: So, it's important that you play the headhunter at their game. Well, not like 'play', more just if you're interested in the job, just tell them. If you're not interested in the job, then tell them as well but don't say, "I don't want this job"; use it as an opportunity to say, "BUT if the following job appears, I'll say yes to that". Because that's useful; then they'll box that in, and then they'll say, "Okay fine", because they're only interested in the "yes" (. . .). So, if you have some doubts = female doubts, just try not to voice them to the headhunter.

In this third interview, Charlotte describes her doubts as 'female'; in an even more explicit example of how feminine qualities are described with disdain and used pejoratively *by women*. This was also highlighted earlier in the way that women's networks were referred to as 'handbag clubs' and how they distance themselves from femininity. It also suggests that she aligns conviction as something more common in men and that women, therefore, need to do more often: disavowing their 'female' doubts and pushing forward. This adopts a 'lean-in' rhetoric *par excellence*; women are encouraged (and encourage themselves) to tackle the internalised barriers (i.e. themselves) that might hold them back: be courageous, strong and push themselves forward, more so than they are already doing. The way that Charlotte uses the phrase 'female doubts' casts it as if it is common sense: an interpretive repertoire that draws on neoliberal feminist discourses, wherein women's difference and self-limiting behaviour are taken for granted and their conviction and self-belief offered as a solution.

ELEANOR [FIRST INTERVIEW]: And then when you follow up [after the interview with the headhunter], you actually pull the job description out and you = they say all the different requirements; you take one or two requirements; you put them in the email, and you give evidence as to why you have got those positions. So, it is like an application form for a university degree, right? You've got to look it that way, you can't just say, "Here's my CV". You've got to preface it, and you have to put in the work.

Like Laura earlier in this chapter, Eleanor compares the board appointment process with other kinds of recruitment, in this case a degree application. By doing so, she draws attention to the similarities between this and other levels of recruitment and discursively takes the responsibility out of the hands of the headhunter and, therefore, away from what is specific to elite recruitment. By describing it in these terms, her insistence that you need to 'put in the work' is explained, and this has a knock-on effect of justifying the process. Given that, in this case, the 'work' she is talking about—identifying what about her background would fit the role—could be seen as the headhunters' responsibility, she discursively reduces their role and their effectiveness to something she has to address. This acts to simultaneously downplay or denigrate the role of the headhunter while also applying self-attribution to the success.

KAREN [FIRST INTERVIEW]: So, we [Karen and the headhunter] were going to meet up, but because it was over Easter, we couldn't. I said, "Well look if you like, I [could] just send you a little note saying why I think my experience fits the brief". And that's what I tend to do if I see anything, you know, to make it easy for the headhunter. Because you can have your CV, but nobody knows it as well as you do, so, therefore, I send it and then say, "You know I fit the brief because of blah, blah, blah", and some of those things will be on the CV, but you can give greater detail, so what I did, so he then said, "Oh that's really helpful, I don't need to meet you then"; literally, I was able to list in each of my roles where I had experience in the area that they said on the specification.

Karen's explanation, like Eleanor and Charlotte's, presents her as working hard to 'manage' the relationship with the headhunter and push herself forward. This 'work' relates to her understanding of how to play the game: recognising how headhunters work, as well as relating it to having the right experience and needing to translate how her experience meets the brief set by the boards and again is an example of a candidate working to make it easy for the headhunter. The headhunter and the CV thus become aspects of the story that are discursively drawn upon as a way for the candidates to make sense of their own success within a highly individualised, neoliberal framework and which affords her the credit for her success too.

Failure and Self-Blame

In one sense, the way that women adopted neoliberal feminist discourses to make sense of their success is understandable, particularly when placed in the wider context of corporate feminism; breaking through the glass ceiling to get very senior roles is treated as 'success' that women have the right to claim some individual credit for. However the adoption of these discourses is perhaps more concerning and pernicious when we saw women also using it to account for their failure (to play the game) as being due to their own failures and character flaws and requiring more work. We saw this emerge in women's accounts of difficulties they faced during their search for roles where they were relatively unsuccessful, where dealing with failure most commonly meant pushing forward and working harder to get a role.

SCARLETT: So how does that frustration make you feel about the search going forward, I mean, have you changed your mind?

MARTHA [SECOND INTERVIEW]: I haven't changed my mind, but I'm trying to think about new or different ways of going about it, you know? Someone said to me early on, "You should identify boards that you want to go after and go speak to some of the people on it". And yeah that's probably not a bad way of doing it: find somebody that knows somebody, that sort of thing. So I need to do that next. But you have to have time to do that.

We see in Martha's account how interviewees adopted the notion that they are required to work hard to make their own success, even when they are not successful. This extract is an example of how candidates' strategies (also seen in the previous chapter's discussion around networking) are discursively used here to make sense of the barriers they face in the process; Martha can raise an issue with the process overall but emphasises the need to find new ways 'around it' rather than challenging it. While Martha describes the situation as frustrating, her 'solution' is to come up with new strategies for targeting specific boards and broadening her network. She identifies the problem as her not having time to network rather than challenging the need to have connections or noting that she does not know the people she is trying to contact. This means adopting an individualised discourse to make sense of her frustration and lack of success, contributing to her feeling that she needs to work harder and find a new way to seek roles. This is seen again in her third interview:

SCARLETT: Has your motivation for doing it waned? Or does it come and go in phases, or?

MARTHA [THIRD INTERVIEW]: No, it hasn't waned at ALL; it's just gotten to a stage where I don't know whether I am (.) frustrated? I'm in a lull? (.) = I'm going to give up? = I'm, you know, I was about to say, I was about to turn negative (.) I do wonder about that. But that's not in my nature; I'm a fighter. I am a fighter. And I get angry with myself, I shouldn't say angry, I get disappointed with myself if I start to think that way. I have to grab hold of the situation and [think], "Look around you, look at how grateful you should be, for everything". So I do that. I force myself to do that. But I am in a bit of a crossroads. I really am. You know, it's either I just give up trying and see what's happening; I do the work with these guys [current employer], and I will continue to network, and if it happens it happens, and if it doesn't it doesn't (.) I'm on the cusp of something, some big change. And the conventional way that I've been trying to do something, which is what this is all about, is so not working, so I've gotta change direction. And I don't know how to do that. And I'm hoping, with these advisors, I might be able to find that path.

In this extract, Martha again seems to internalise her failure, describing it in terms of pathological or negative emotions: the frustration she feels in relation to the process and her lack of success. She discursively treats her emotions as something she has to address in the appropriate way by coming up with more practical 'solutions' and continuing to push for roles. The evocation of herself as a fighter who has to battle and continue to work hard is a starkly neoliberal discourse, particularly in its reference to her need to be 'grateful' for what she has achieved thus far and continuing to try different strategies to work around the system rather than challenging the need to conduct these strategies. Martha also describes a kind of 'meta-shame' (Probyn, 2005): she feels angry or frustrated *because* she is angry and frustrated, and in the interview, she seems to be encouraging herself to handle these emotions in a more appropriate way.

Charlotte similarly describes her feelings of frustration with the process:

CHARLOTTE [SECOND INTERVIEW]: So, I think (.) I'm feeling that I'm resigned to (.) it's just going to take a lot of time? (.) and you've just got to keep plugging away at it. But there are moments when you just go, "God, this is so hard". Is it really the right thing to do? But I don't want to ditch (.) I feel like I've ditched, you know, being CEO of a FTSE 100 because I don't want to do that anymore, and it's all that I'd ever wanted in my life (.) and now something that just feels that it's quite difficult, I think I've just got to keep plugging away at it but it's um. It is VERY difficult, more difficult than I thought. Because there's no road map, you don't actually know and there's not (.) there doesn't seem to be any (.) there's NO RULES.

Charlotte, like Martha, explains her frustration with the process in relation to the work she has still to do. She emphasises her determination to keep pushing forward even while describing how difficult and opaque the process is; the solution she presents is to keep working, even while there is a lack of certainty that this is what will lead to success. This is justified further in her account by the insistence that it is going to take a lot of time and hard work—a discourse that is mobilised alongside a contradiction that the process is unpredictable, and she does not know how to navigate it because there are 'no rules'. The internalisation of failure in Charlotte's account also emerges in how she references her previous decision to 'ditch' being a CEO of a FTSE 100, using this to reaffirm her determination to continue 'plugging away' to get a non-executive board role.

Neoliberal feminism has both the effect of converting gender equality into personal responsibility and conflating equality with getting more women into positions of power. It is a call to arms to women to strive to reach the top of their organisations and demand a 'seat at the table' but one that only offers the revolutionary tools of 'confidence' (Gill and Orgad, 2016) and self-actualised, individuated progression rather than solidarity and equality. This is particularly problematic because, in part, drawing on a presumed linear narrative of progress (Foster, 2016), it 'assumes that the revolution has in some sense already taken place, and therefore all women need to do is to rouse themselves by absorbing and acting on this reality' (Rottenberg, 2014: p. 426).

When describing their experiences of the appointment process overall and making sense of their relative successes and failures, women in this study draw on these neoliberal feminist discourses. Their narratives place them as female heroes, battling against their internal barriers (both bodily and mentally or emotionally) to push for board roles and make their own success. This is often couched in terms of their ability to persist, learning the rules of the game and how to play by them. Additionally, this relates their individualised success story to their ability to network and get appointed rather than specifically to a meritocratic discourse where they are simply the best person for the role, recruited through a rational or objective process. This has the discursive effect of downplaying bias and the struggles they face in the process: either pre-empting or not allowing space for criticism of the process.

Sitting Back

In contrast to the neoliberal feminist 'lean-in' discourse that the women commonly adopted, men drew on a 'sit-back' discourse to account for their success and failure. They rarely described success as something they actively sought or pushed for, instead emphasising how they were approached by appointing boards and putting emphasis on how 'out of the blue' the connections were made or the (apparently) little effort they had put in.

SIMON [SECOND INTERVIEW]: And one night I got a phone call (.) from somebody at [search firm] funnily enough ^about six o'clock I think^ and, "I know you don't know me, but I would like to talk to you about a possible job". Long story short, I went to see him at their offices in Mayfair and the largest glass of scotch I remember seeing in quite some time. We sat down in this room, a very comfortable room, and they pitched the [company name] job to me, and I liked the sound of it very much indeed, and I then I accepted it or interviewed da de da did the process and got offered the job at [company name]. So (.) I took that, obviously (.).

The language Simon uses to describe how he was contacted for a board role evokes two key discourses: that of elite identity and of the informality in the process. The 'offices in Mayfair' and the 'large glass of scotch' are markers of traditional Old Boys' networks or gentleman's clubs; characteristics typically associated with 'gentlemanly capitalism' (Augar, 2008). He also points to the informality in the process by emphasising how comfortable he was and how seemingly unexpected it all was. In contrast to women's accounts, Simon does not have any active role in how he describes it; rather, he is a passive recipient of success. This also comes through in his emphasising that the headhunter did not know him before making contact. It is interesting that here not being known to the headhunter is used as a means to emphasise his high status or success, while for others, not being known to the right people is presented as a significant barrier.

The difference between how Simon describes the actions and behaviours of the headhunter and how women in this research describe them is also notable. In the women's accounts we described earlier, the headhunter is treated as passive and needing people (women) to do the work for them: a resource that can be accessed but only if they themselves put in the work. In Simon's account, the headhunter contacts him out of the blue and offers him a role. Placing this in the wider contextual research on headhunters we described in Chapter 2, this may suggest that men's accounts of the relationship between candidates and headhunters is more aligned with how headhunters themselves describe the relationship, as they are not typically interested in candidates who approach them (cf. Beaverstock *et al.*, 2015; Holgersson, 2013; Wirz, 2014). It also suggests that men may not feel they need to emphasise their 'work' in the same way women do.

Simon's account also provides an example of how interviewees, although most frequently men, were vague in describing the specific stages of the board appointment process and often reluctant to provide details. In Simon's account, for example, he starts by saying he has accepted the role and then almost immediately qualifies this by saying he 'interviewed' for it, despite there being little discussion of an interview, and providing little explanation as to what the interview process entailed. His use of the phrase 'da de da' also acts as a way for him to brush over or actively avoid discussing the steps of the appointment process; he dismisses it as unimportant for discussion despite it being the focus of the research. The overall effect is that he conflates his decision to take the role with their decision to appoint him, implying that once he decided he was interested, he was, seemingly immediately, appointed.

IAN [FIRST INTERVIEW]: I happened just to mention [that I am looking] to a friend of mine who happened to be the senior partner of one of the major law firms—a guy I was at university with and who was a personal friend. He happened to be talking with [a board] whom they advised (. . .). They used him as a little bit, as companies do, and it's interesting, actually, they just asked him, they said, "We've got a chairman retiring"; someone was becoming chairman, and they had a spare role on the board. What they needed really was someone from the city. (. . .) He just so happened to say, "Funny you should say that, but my friend [Ian], who by the way comes from very close to [town where the company is based], just said that he's been look-ing and would like to look at something". So he put me in touch with them, and I went down. To this day, I laugh because it's the type of company I really enjoy because we had the interview in a pub,[1] and I thought that was a great way to start. I think they were traditional [industry]; I was this strange four-tailed, two-headed chap from the city, and we got on like a house on fire.

In Ian's account, we see similar references made to the informality in the process: the conversation that led to the appointment was held in a pub, and, again, the emphasis is placed on how comfortable and enjoyable he found it. It is also notable here, even more so than with Simon, that he refers throughout to luck and happenstance: Ian repeatedly states that he 'happened to' mention he was looking for a role, and his friend 'hap-pened to' know someone who could offer him something suitable. This discourse acts as a way of eliding the networked connections that led to the meeting arising, ascribing the success to a series of coincidences rather than the active and deliberate actions of the three people (men) involved. Like Simon, Ian's description of the interview and success is fairly short: 'He put me in touch with them and I went down (. . .) we got on like a house on fire'. This is a discursive attempt to reduce the interview process to a minimal explanation. This also downplays the active role the can-didate has in the process and, again, ascribes success to something that happens *to* him rather than as a result of his deliberate and active seeking.

In a similar way that we found women used 'leaning in' to make sense of both their successes and their failures, men used this 'sitting-back' discourse to explain why they had not (yet) been successful in getting a board role. This provided a way for the men to make sense of not yet being successful and to retrospectively and proactively justify their net-working practices.

SCARLETT: So do you have any kind of plan for how you're going to move forward from here?
ANTHONY [THIRD INTERVIEW]: I've never really been a planner I think (.) really milling around is what does it.

SCARLETT: So that will be the plan?

ANTHONY: Yeah. Do a lot of milling around. [I did] management by milling around, business development by milling around, portfolio by
milling around. And, actually, the 'milling about process' and the
being patient and knowing it will come to you seems to be a much
more effective way of getting on boards. Provided you are of the calibre that is going to be approached and once you are in the band of
being, "Yes that person has the right level of experience", you actually do just seem to have to bob around, being in the right spaces,
existing in the world until the right position comes up for you, and
then it will come, and you will be the right one for it.

In response to questions concerning his planning, Anthony draws on a
'sitting-back' discourse by saying he will be 'milling around': a kind of
mantra that he uses to make sense of the process overall, which he places
seemingly in opposition to planning. He starts by asserting that milling
around is 'what does it', connecting his personal strategy to an assertion
that it will lead to success, in a similar way that we saw from women
earlier in this chapter but used here specifically in opposition to my use
of the word 'plan', which he deliberately avoids. In both his rejection of
planning and his insistence that success comes from 'milling around', he
refers both to his career background and to an internal sense of self or
subjectivity to assert that it is the best way of going about the process: not
only is it the best route to non-exec success but also it is part of 'who he
is'. Similarly, by stating that he has *never* been a planner, he implies that
throughout his entire career, successes have come from 'milling around'
and not planning. This, then, combines an internal subjectivity, his perspective on what has led to success in his career and his attitudes towards
the search for a role all under the same rubric: being patient, not needing
to push forward and success coming to him.

This is similar to the discourses that emerged in how men make sense
of their networking practices, where they stated that sitting back and
being patient was the best way to get a role, and in this way, the men
present themselves as deliberately passive. Rather than articulating this
as a deliberate strategy, however, it is described as something they do
unconsciously, as part of 'who they are'. This contrasts with the women's
accounts, where they outline specific strategies that they have learned
to 'play the game'. Their discourses present the process as a result of
passivity that they perform unconsciously, a notably different discursive
strategy to women.

It is also important to highlight that the sitting back discourse necessarily relies upon a conviction that the individual mobilising it believes
(or wishes to emphasise) that he will eventually be appointed; it does
not challenge the conviction that he has in the likelihood of his success.
Anthony states that success is about 'knowing' the opportunity will

come to you, which he relates to having the right *level* of experience. This, again, uses the right experience discourse described in Chapter 2 to explain why someone would be successful and connects it to the person (i.e. him) being the right calibre of person. As in Simon's discussion earlier regarding his success, he presents himself as in an elite position, with the director role seen as a foregone conclusion or *sine qua non*: a taken-for-granted part of his career that will come and for which he just has to be patient. This is in stark contradiction to the women's highly strategic networking strategies and their sense making, where success is attributed to hard work, and failure motivates them to push harder to get roles. This does not allow discursive space for any notion of failure. Failure, in the men's narratives, is cast as success that has not happened yet or as the result of a deliberate decision to approach things slowly.

Being Choosy

Another way that interviewees used the 'sitting back' discourse was by describing themselves as 'choosy' about which roles they would pursue or take, explaining that they had not been successful because they had only been interested in a small number of roles relative to how many they were approached about.

SCARLETT: So apart from phone calls, have you had any other short-listings or interviews for positions that you then didn't get?
STEPHEN [SECOND INTERVIEW]: Things did start flowing. I didn't pursue any, as I said, there was [*sic*] two in particular I was eager to pursue but ruled them out, so I was very picky. The only interview process I went through, getting in front of a company, was [company name]. (. . .) So, a hundred percent success rate I guess, you could say. (. . .) So and a nought percent failure rate. But you know, it's kind of like that. No, it's not kind of like that, I could, it might not have worked, and I would have bided my time for something else.

Stephen was particularly elusive about his experiences of seeking roles and frequently adopted a 'sitting-back' discourse to explain his experiences. In describing his overall perception of the process and his search for roles, he presents himself as being very selective in what kinds of roles he wants, emphasising both his 'choosiness' and his 'patience'. His insistence in the interview that 'things did start flowing' but that he 'didn't pursue any' of these opportunities is mobilised seemingly to suggest that being interviewed or shortlisted for (only) two roles was a decision he made rather than representing a lack of success. Despite explicitly asking him about other positions and in the interview attempting to move away from discussing his success with the role he got, he repeatedly brought the conversation back to the roles he did get. This is most notable in this extract where he describes his 'hundred percent success rate' (and a 'nought percent failure rate' to reaffirm the point), presenting the relatively few approaches he has had as a sign of his *success* and his decision to be choosy. Similarly, he describes hypothetically how he might not have been successful but here casts himself as being patient, stating that if it had not led to success, he would have 'bided his time' for something else. In terms of how he describes the process, he does not blame the system for his lack of success nor does he locate it as his responsibility. It is internalised only insofar as it is as a result of his decision to be picky, not to the extent that he is taking personal responsibility for success or failure and without challenging the notion that he will be successful and is a desirable candidate for board roles.

Other interviewees also described being choosy but for different reasons:

DANIEL [SECOND INTERVIEW]: I mean, so they have got to be sure that it's building the right (.) so I have had one meeting, two meetings with the CEO, I am in the middle of doing due diligence now on them and their finances and structure and issues to decide whether it's a job that I want to do. Since you are personally liable, and your reputation is (.) and for me—because it is the first one—who I choose, I mean I have got to be realistic of this size and reputation given my background, but I have also got to make sure that I don't get into bed with somebody who is not going to be well thought of or is already not well thought of because that doesn't help.

In this extract, Daniel explains specifically why he felt he needed to be choosy when deciding whether to take on a board role he was being considered for, relating it to personal liability and reputation, something he sees as more important because it is his first position. This, again, draws on the ideal board member discourse we discussed earlier, as it connects his need to be 'realistic' with his level of experience and shows the strength of the previous board experience discourse for making sense of the process and for providing an interpretive repertoire for his identity. This also may be mobilised as a form of self-affronting justification for failure before the fact, presenting an explanation for why he might not 'choose' a role even if he is offered one (even before he has been offered one). The need to be choosy is counteracted by his perception of himself as someone with no previous experience, with the inference that not having previous board experience means that he cannot be choosy or as choosy as he would like to be. Even within this small extract, he describes the process as him being approached and deciding what he wants rather than him actively seeking roles. The concern with his reputation also forms part of the narrative.

SCARLETT: Is that something that you were advised on as well about being choosy about who you go for? Was that advice from people who had been through it?

GARY [THIRD INTERVIEW]: Yes. It was unhelpful advice, but it's (.): well, you need to get the balance right; you need to recognise the realities of [the situation]; you need to get the first one because it turns out when you are on 'the circuit', as they like to call it, you get phoned up. So you need to be realistic about what you have got, what the skills are, what you are likely to get, but you also need to make sure you don't get involved with a deadbeat. And, you know, you have to come to that conclusion by your own due diligence, you know? Does this smell right? Does it feel right?

Similarly to Daniel, Gary's explanations of the process here emphasise the need to be choosy to ensure that he is not taking on a role that is unsuitable or that he is not completely sure they wanted. Both acknowledged that there was a need to be realistic: these are not the same explicitly self-assured discourses we saw in Simon, Ian and Stephen. However, they still adopted this sitting back discourse that allowed them to present themselves as able to choose the role that suited them. The way they describe how they go about 'due diligence' on companies they are interested in is similar to characteristics of 'fit' discussed in the earlier chapter: Gary's description of a company 'smelling' or 'feeling right' uses highly informal language and is vague about what exactly he is looking for; similarly, while Daniel discusses due diligence in relation to finances and structure, he then uses a colloquial expression ('I don't [want to] get into bed with somebody who is not going to be well thought of'). Both of these descriptions present the decision as important, but one that is done almost on 'gut instinct' or a feeling about a company, something often seen in other studies with regard to how directors are appointed and which reflect the findings of this research too. This, again, reaffirms Gary's sense of self-belief, as it relies on a conviction that he is able to judge the value of the board simply by instinct. This suggests that while there is some reliance on having the right experience or being the right kind of company, when it comes to the final decision making, it is done largely on informal assessment.

Although the 'sitting-back' discourse was used almost exclusively by men, it was occasionally used by women who had found it easy to get roles. Here Linda describes a concern that she had taken on too many.

LINDA [SECOND INTERVIEW]: [If I get those two] I'm full, at least for a year until I've BEDDED DOWN. They bombard you with offers, and you've gotta make judgements (.) I've got a little bit of consultancy, some bits and pieces, happy to do that. If I don't get the other two, I would probably, probably still sit there and see what comes to me. Because the, I'm seeing [headhunter] this afternoon and I know they're going to say the same as the chap at [headhunter] said, which is "wait". Sit back. Because the difference between exec and non-executive is rotations. Now, if I use up my dance card all in one go, let's say that even if I wanted to, which I don't, but if [company] came up to me next May and said, "We're looking for a chair or even a member", I wouldn't be able to do it because I'll have filled my portfolio, and I'll have finished them within five years. So I'm having to sit back and go, okay, stop.

The way that Linda describes this need to 'sit back', be choosy and make sure she is taking on the right kinds of roles is similar in its outcome to that of Daniel and Gary in the sense that she acknowledges the need to 'be choosy'. This is presented as advice provided by a headhunter. Her justification for this is different than in their accounts: in Linda's case, it is related to her success, describing her as being in high demand and, therefore, needing to make sure she does not fill her portfolio too quickly, preventing her from taking other roles. A 'dance card' is a colloquial expression referring to a tradition where a woman's dance card was used to record the names of the gentlemen with whom she intended to dance with at a formal ball; someone's dance card being full implies that even though they are interested, they have no time slots for another person. For Linda, the need to 'be choosy' is, therefore, strategic in the sense that she does not want to fill her portfolio too quickly (and be unable to take on other roles) rather than seeking to present herself as a discerning person. The way her discourse is mobilised is different than men's; it is also highly gendered imagery in which the woman holds the dance card and waits to be approached by (presumably eager) men. Linda's choosiness, rather than being a strategy to increase her chances of success in getting the role in the way that men describe, is still compatible with her 'lean-in' discourse, despite her choice of imagery.

'It's Easier for Women'

Another discourse that men drew on to make sense of the process and that also relates to the 'sit-back' discourse was the assertion that it is easier for women than men to get roles. This was exclusively attributed to the women-on-boards agenda that was prominent in the UK at the time.

ANTHONY [SECOND INTERVIEW]: I also think, I'm just going to have to wait it out. Whilst positions come up; there are a lot of them; there is a lot of supply, ^a lot of supply^.

SCARLETT: Is that something you feel, that actually there is a lot of people in a similar position to you?

ANTHONY: ^Oh yeah, there is a lot of people, a lot of people^, either because they are in my position or because they have decided to step away ^from being on the executive side^; they may have been encouraged to do it by the company they're in. There is a lot of different reasons. And it's also about relevant knowledge as well. The guy last night, [name], he is on the board of [FTSE 100 company], and that's something that [Fortune 500[2] company] have supported him with and helped him with so you know, there's (.) you can see how he would fit and bring a different perspective into a board room from a technology aspect point of view. So the longer it goes on for me (.) what are you bringing to the board?

SCARLETT: So, I suppose in that way it's good that you still have the full-time role and that you are still very current?

ANTHONY: Well, that would be (.) the remuneration is quite, it's a major part of what I do. That's something that you can kind of latch on to and say, "Well, that's my area of expertise".

SCARLETT: Yeah, of course, which makes you quite an easy candidate for it?

ANTHONY: Yes, for certain types of roles. But then they come up, so say there is a chair of a remuneration committee; what's the candidate list like, and that's an easy place to get a female. So then you come back to the start point again.

In the beginning of this extract, Anthony uses the sit back discourse in relation to being patient, stating specifically that he needs to 'wait it out' because of the increased number of candidates now looking for roles. This idea of a 'swelled pool' was common in men's and women's narratives, and for many, it was related to an assertion that in recent years there are many more aspiring non-executive directors looking for roles; here Anthony refers to it as another external explanation to account for him having not gained a role yet. This reaffirms his conviction that he will be successful by placing the blame on a factor he cannot control (and one that, we should point out, cannot be verified). This initial assertion that there are more candidates than before is gender neutral; he does not start by stating there are more women. It is notable, therefore, that he then moves the discussion to his area of expertise ('it's also about relevant knowledge') and suggests he has not been successful due to not fitting a specific niche before finally stating that remuneration committee chair is an 'easy place to get a female'. To account for his thus far lack of success he therefore draws on both the right experience and an easier for women discourse, as well as stating that there are, in general, too many aspiring directors. In contrast to the women's accounts early in this chapter, Anthony's reasons are all factors outside his control, insinuating that his lack of success is due to boards needing to get women onto boards, and to a presumption that the remuneration chair is an 'easy' place for them to do that.

STEPHEN [SECOND INTERVIEW]: They [headhunters and NED peers] all said, "You're just the right credentials for the chairman of audit committee, that you should, you know, find this (.) you'll find the right thing, just give it time" (. . .). I was kind of a pretty decent candidate, the only (.) as I said, the only one bit of feedback that stuck in my mind was and it wasn't feedback, it was sort of an opinion or anecdote or whatever-

SCARLETT: Yeah, of course.

STEPHEN: [They said] "If you were a woman, you would be walking straight in".

SCARLETT: Yeah, absolutely.

STEPHEN: And give it time.

It is striking how Stephen, in a similar way to Anthony, simultaneously relates his conviction that he will be successful to his experience and career background, while also affirming that his failure so far is a result of the increased focus on getting women into roles. Much like the men's accounts already noted, he has conviction in his own ability and relates that to his experience of being highly desired by boards; his career background represents the 'right experience'. His lack of success in getting a NED role is distinct from his own success narrative. His mobilisation of this discourse is direct and explicit; rather, than hinting at a preference for women as Anthony did, he states outright that if he was a woman, he would be 'walking straight in', evoking an idea that there *are* women walking straight into such roles and that he has been told this by a headhunter. This downplays the at times convoluted, opaque and time-consuming appointment process, and maintains that the only thing preventing him from securing a role is that he is not a woman.

BENJAMIN [THIRD INTERVIEW]: So, I started looking in that sort of time frame and it was pretty tough (.) Pretty tough for men to get roles within that time frame. One very well-known city headhunter, female, said to me, "Ben, if you wore a skirt, I'd get you to any boardroom you want, any day (.) but at the minute, there's a flood of women being recruited. Bide your time; you'll get the right appointment". That really sums up the mood during that time because there was that big push (.) there was the Davies' report and (.) was other committees and things that came out.

SCARLETT: Yes, of course.

BENJAMIN: And it was predominantly or significantly female-focused recruitment at the time. So, positive recruitment. Positive discrimination.

Again, we see the role that patience and sitting back plays in men's accounts and the strong insistence that it is, at this time, much easier for women. It should be highlighted that during the time frame Benjamin is referring to, 70% of new board roles in the FTSE 350 were given to men, while women may have been more sought out than in previous years, they were not, and never have been, taking the majority of appointments.

The stress he places on the headhunter being female is also notable, seeming to point out that women also think boards are looking for women, perhaps to suggest that it is not just his opinion and not just the opinion of men. Benjamin's interviews also show us how the Davies' review and women on boards were viewed retrospectively as a distinct period of time that just had to be waited out rather than indicative of long-lasting change. His describing it as 'that time frame' again indicates that it is related to the need to appoint women in order to satisfy a quota or meet the target: he refers explicitly to the Davies' review as an instigator for 'female-focused' recruitment. He then even more explicitly calls it positive discrimination—a loaded phrase that places it within diversity and inclusion rhetoric and language (Noon, 2007) but drawing on its negative connotations to criticise its effects.

Andrew draws on a similar narrative to Benjamin, although in his account, it was another NED who told him it would be easier to get a role if he were a woman:

ANDREW [SECOND INTERVIEW]: He [another NED] said why don't we have lunch and discuss it, so this was more initially for me to say, "You know the market; you know how people choose NEDs; here is my background. Is it feasible to imagine that there's enough interest in someone like me to find some NED roles?" And the feedback was, one, it's a pity you're not a woman because, frankly, there's (.) a bias at that point because boards are completely unrepresented in that regard, and that means that it is nothing to do with your background particularly, but the focus is so much for a re-balance because many people are not interested in more eclectic, risky candidates because their first problem is that they don't have a balanced board.

Like Linda's account of her husband earlier in the chapter, and Stephen and Anthony's description of the headhunter's feedback, it is notable how throughout the research, candidates use other people in their narratives as mouthpieces or representatives to explain their perspective, and in this case as a way to back up their belief that it is easier for women. Discursively, this makes it easier for them to describe and may also be a way to defend against perceived criticism, claiming it is not necessarily their opinion, just something they have been told. As with Stephen, Andrew reiterates that there is no problem with his background (i.e. his ability to get board roles), again reiterating the idea of the ideal board member and drawing on the right experience discourse but relates his difficulty to not being a woman and that relates to the boards need to 're-balance'. This need is not necessarily criticised; his account acknowledges that lack of balance needs to be addressed, and he is, therefore, not challenging the system *per se* but rather how it affects him. In contrast to Stephen, whose experience and background fits the 'ideal board member' described earlier, Andrew found his experience less typically desired for boards (he was the candidate who described putting his HR experience into a 'business' perspective in Chapter 3) and hence his conviction that he is a riskier or more 'eclectic' candidate. Even so, in this narrative, the need for boards to appoint women is the overriding discourse and reason for his lack of success; this, therefore, becomes the primary failure narrative despite contradicting other difficulties he faces.

In relation to the belief that it is easier for women due to the focus on board diversity, it was remarkable how the men incorporated this belief into their narratives while also espousing support for board diversity.

ANTHONY [SECOND INTERVIEW]: I have to say I'm fairly philosophical because I absolutely support the idea that we need more females on board, you know. I've seen that, and I have to acknowledge probably that over the duration of my career, which is 36 years, that men have probably had the advantage, so now the pendulum has now swung the other way, well good on the females. But that is something that obviously I am wrestling with. I almost sort of feel that if I was a woman at this point, I probably would have been welcomed with open arms, and they would have seen through my perceived lack of corporate board responsibilities, and I would probably (.) have two or three non-executive roles lined up already. (.) So, that's just an added frustration, but as I say, I am philosophical about the whole thing.

Anthony's insistence that he is positive about the need to increase the number of women on boards is particularly striking in how it is mobilised here alongside an insistence that it is easier for women and relating that to his lack of success so far. Here he uses an A-B-A discursive structure— being positive, then negative, then positive about women getting more roles. This structure has been observed in other studies that explore how men talk about feminism (Riley, 2003), and it acts as a disclaimer (Gill, 2000; Hewitt and Stokes, 1975): attempting to offer a criticism while seemingly being aware that he must portray himself as positive about getting more women onto boards. Like Andrew, he acknowledges that there may be challenges with his experience; however, in this particular extract from a later interview, he now implies that the career background would be unimportant if he were a woman. This again represents a complex contradiction between the discourses of meritocracy and bias that is difficult to resolve in candidates' accounts.

GARY [SECOND INTERVIEW]: What we've got at the moment, actually, again, I'm a straight talker; I just like things said as they are (.) What we've done is we've actually changed the rules for admission of non-execs in order to have more women on the board because there's not enough. And by the way, it's always difficult to get an executive director because they're so busy. I mean, we had one on a board I'm on, and she's heroic; I don't know how she has the time. I have no idea; there's times when she has to leave the board meeting and take calls and all that sort of stuff, so it's very, very hard. And I think what we've done, we've taken people out of the legal profession and the accounting profession, which never used to be considered as necessary for the board because they do different things; they don't run businesses. We've taken people out of the charity sector; we've taken people who are lower down the hierarchy and that sort, and you know what I'm saying? I'm saying that is fine by me because actually that is quite interesting.

The way that Gary draws on the easier for women discourse is slightly different than the others discussed in this section, partly because he gained a FTSE 100 NED role during the research period, and it is, therefore, not being mobilised to make sense of failure; however, it is notable that the strength of the discourse is similar even when the discourse is used for a different function. In this account, he hints at a criticism of the women-on-boards agenda overall for how it has changed the composition of boards, arguing that it has meant the appointment of candidates with less experience or from 'lower down the hierarchy'. Caveating his statement at the beginning with 'I'm a straight talker' suggests, again, that he is applying a disclaimer before he says it, in a similar discursive structure to other men's. The anecdote about the woman he sits on a board with is an interesting segue in his story: by highlighting her ability to be a good director, he singles her out as an example of how successful women can be as directors, but she is presented as an anomaly or 'superwoman', which 'others' or singles out her experience. It is also notable that the reasons he gives for her being 'heroic' are centred on her ability to balance an executive role and a non-executive role, something that is common across the FTSE and done by both men and women. That he praises her ability to do both, again, acts to single her out, offering praise (perhaps patronisingly) for doing something that it is normal for a director to do.

While Gary does not use the easier-for-women discourse to make sense of his own failure, he highlights a belief that the increased appointment of women has changed the kinds of people taken on for board roles; this suggests another aspect of the right experience discourse, where he states that people who have the 'wrong' experience are now being appointed and that this is as a result of the focus on women. The implication that women are, by nature, further down the 'hierarchy' amounts to, arguably, sexist criticism and again relates a wider (negative) change to the women-on-boards agenda. This is then notably caveated or sandwiched, again using the A-B-A structure (Riley, 2003) as in Anthony's account, to state that it is 'fine by him' because it makes it more 'interesting'. His overall narrative is highly contradictory: he is critical of the influence of the women-on-boards agenda because it leads to the rules of admission changing while maintaining that it is, overall, a good thing.

GARY [THIRD INTERVIEW]: In many ways, I think it's actually quite, quite refreshing to have that (.) different view. But you have to recognise it's a different set of experiences. And is it what a board wants? You know? I just think, so with the [company] thing, if you had had someone who's not been on a board before, who, say, came out of a law firm or charity or not-for-profit sector, would they have been able to deliver a message about the management of that company? And have the courage to stick to that? And do you know what? I'm not saying "no" on that. I'm saying, you know, I think you probably get that MORE out of someone who has been through the rough and tumble of getting to the top of a company and being an executive and being on boards, as you will from somebody who has not been in that kind of slightly rough-and-tumble private sector. But that's what we've done, but I personally welcome it.

Gary's narrative in the third interview around the same issue is remarkably similar to his second interview, again suggesting that it acts as a resource that he draws on to make sense of the process and repeats in the research interview. In this extract, he uses the same discursive structure, stating that it is 'refreshing' to have a different point of view but that it is a necessarily different view before going on to offer an example of a board where this might not work. The example he offered was a high-profile governance failure, and his implication is that someone who does not have the 'right experience' may not be able to challenge the executive directors. This again draws on the right experience discourse but connects it with the right personality, constructing an overall rationality that people who are not 'ideal' in terms of their experience will not be able to be good directors. Again, we see the discursive shift and contradictions between raising it as a potential problem and contradicting the narrative by saying that he 'isn't saying "no"' in a remarkably similar way as the disclaimer 'I'm not being sexist, but . . .' Gill (2000) finds in her research. Finally, the account ends with another iteration of the same discursive structure: he raises a problem with the process before concluding that he 'welcomes' the change. Overall, these accounts suggest awareness that it is socially unacceptable to be opposed to women on boards (and indeed this is likely influenced by the knowledge that women on boards was the subject of the research) but also wanting to explain a negative effect of increased appointment of women.

Conclusion

This chapter has explored how candidates make sense of the overall appointment process and in particular their own success and failure. This reveals how candidates use gendered discourses to explain the process and how it operates, as well as how these have enduring, discursive effects on how the process is perceived and maintained.

We have seen how women's accounts of success and failure draw on neoliberal feminist discourses. Women seeking roles often describe themselves as having battled against both internal and external barriers in order to be successful. Internally, their accounts often contained examples of feeling uncomfortable or unsure and facing a challenge but explaining how they pushed forward and 'battled through', ultimately leading to success. This is also seen in how they describe the external barriers they tackled through 'playing the system'—for instance, by making the process easy for the headhunters or being active in their networking. This presents the process as something that is undesirable (and at times 'pointless') but also necessary and the inevitable route to success. By characterising it as such, they are criticising the process without challenging it. The way candidates draw on these narratives also portrays them as highly active and instrumental in creating the circumstances for their success, drawing on a neoliberal, self-responsibility framework where they are the creators of their own successes.

Women in the research also used similar discourses to make sense of failure; often, the difficulties they were facing caused a great deal of frustration and negative feelings towards the process and how it operates. The reliance on networking for roles presents a dilemma for unsuccessful candidates, as the only solution they have is to 'lean in' and network harder or more, with little access to boards through other routes. The intangibility of success and lack of 'map' or 'rules' was particularly evident in women's accounts: they expressed a desire to push forward and work harder, but a lack of clarity about what that could entail. This means that any challenge or critique of the process and how it operates was silenced. Instead, women often described difficulties or challenges they faced getting roles as personal failures. They present solutions and plans for continuing to search for roles, continuing to place the responsibility for success and failure on themselves, with the only solution being to work harder or smarter.

These neoliberal discourses are reminiscent of those presented in corporate feminist 'lean in'-esque texts (Rottenberg, 2014, 2018), which encourage women to break through the glass ceiling by tackling internal barriers, such as lack of confidence or conviction in their own abilities. This rhetoric has been criticised, as it implies that women can overcome barriers provided they have knowledge and internal conviction and are prepared to work hard (Foster, 2016) rather than challenging where the barriers come from. Director recruitment may be a specific circumstance where women internalise the expectation that they create their own success as they go through the process. As critics of corporate feminism have noted, these seemingly feminist discourses have been co-opted by capitalist and neoliberal ideals, and this has the effect of placing the responsibility for failure back on individual women, detracting from the potential for systemic or structural change. Given that the non-executive director recruitment is marked by its gender biases and opacity, it is problematic to see women adopting these issues as their own if it is preventing them from challenging the issues inherent in the system.

These discourses are also, problematically and persistently, meritocratic. Women use highly individualised narratives to emphasise how they achieved success on their own terms by explaining how they have learned what will lead to success and thus 'play the system'. This locates their behaviour within a meritocratic framework (by highlighting that they work hard for their success) but only in relation to learning the rules of the appointment process. Women very rarely related their success or failures to their background, experience or ability to be a good director. Rather than this representing a meritocracy where the roles go to the best candidates, then, this suggests that the roles go to the candidates who work the hardest *within* the appointment process; women can, therefore, succeed, provided they learn the rules of the game and work hard to do so rather than challenging the rules themselves.

Much like the discourses that candidates used to describe networking practices in the previous chapter, we see a stark contrast between women's highly active accounts and men's very passive accounts of the appointment process. This is interestingly counterintuitive, as normally, activity is associated with masculinity and passivity with femininity in career narratives (Kelan, 2009b). Men's accounts made sense of their success through 'sitting back' and not pushing for roles: instead, they described being found, being patient and being choosy. When depicting how they had been recruited to roles, men rarely described their active role in the process, instead using narratives that outlined how they were contacted directly by headhunters or boards and then appointed. In contrast to the women's detailed accounts of the stages of the appointment process, men also described a highly informal process. The emphasis on informality was particularly notable, as this separates it significantly from the expectations of a 'normal' job interview, while women frequently drew parallels between director appointments and other areas of recruitment (something which similarly justifies the process operating as it does). This has the overall effect of emphasising signifiers of men's elite status and the unique aspects of elite recruitment, placing themselves in positions of power and as individuals who are contacted for roles rather than the other way around.

The contradiction and co-existence of active and passive sense making is particularly notable with regard to gender, as it is an inversion of the typical gendered expectations. Particularly in relation to the workplace and leadership, men are commonly seen as pushing forward and more active and direct and women less able to do so. One suggestion for the inversion in this case is that already acknowledged earlier: the encouragement given to women to be more 'like men' in their leadership and networking styles may lead to their pushing themselves forward and 'leaning in' as a deliberate choice to go against the norms of their gender. With regard to the men, this passiveness in relation to the appointment process is attributed to several factors—their emphasis on being found, being patient and being choosy—and these all emphasise their elite status. As with the women's accounts, this same discourse was used by successful candidates, as well as those who had not yet been successful as a way to explain their plans for continuing to search.

While women's failure narratives frequently referred to the work they had to continue to put in, men simply accounted for their lack of success as either relating to their decision to be choosy about roles or their need to be patient and wait for the right role to come to them, both of which rest on the notion that they are right for roles and will, eventually, be successful. Often, this was couched in terms that related to their internal subjectivity: they were more likely to describe leaning back as being unconscious or part of 'who they are'. This allows them a way to maintain 'face'; in the interviews, they portray themselves as not 'really trying' to get roles, while women emphasise how they work hard or need to work harder. Men attribute their lack of success (so far) to their decision to network 'patiently' ('correctly') rather than trying a strategy and that strategy failing/not leading to success.

A final discourse that candidates drew on to make sense of their experiences was the insistence that it was easier for women than men due to the political focus on getting more women onto boards. While some women mentioned this in relation to their motivations for seeking board roles (saying, for instance, that they were seeking roles because there is currently more of a chance for women, so they wanted to seize the opportunity), nearly all the men in this research used it to make sense of their experiences, particularly the difficulties they face. The iteration that it is easier for women to be appointed is often mobilised alongside a conviction in their own success through emphasising how credible a candidate they are and arguing that it is *only* the preference for women that is acting as a barrier to their success, and all they need to do is be patient.

The strength with which and frequency that men insisted it is easier for women (despite more roles still going to men) was startling. It was typically treated as an inevitable result of the board gender targets set by Lord Davies in 2011, but the emphasis on patience may suggest that the focus on women directors would only be short term and only last until the focus dropped. It was also interesting how criticisms of the effect of board diversity initiatives were discussed tentatively; often, this meant the candidate stressing that they were very positive about board diversity before offering a criticism or suggesting a negative effect that it was presumed to have. These ranged from the changing composition of boards to the increased pool of potential candidates or to references to women getting a great number of roles to satisfy the quota, but they were often concluded with an assurance that it was still a 'good thing'. This couching of gendered critique within a politically correct framework is common in men discussing feminist issues (Riley, 2003) and particularly in relation to the workplace, where diversity issues are often discussed very positively in certain areas while denigrated in others (Kelan, 2014).

Perhaps most problematically, the insistence that it is easier for women than men to get board roles has the enduring discursive effect of portraying women's success as primarily the result of board diversity targets rather than related to their own ability or value as directors. This, like the 'lean-in' and 'sit-back' narratives that candidates use to make sense of the process, act as discursive distractions from the problems with the appointment process. The combination of these discourses as used to make sense of the process allows candidates to draw on certain aspects of meritocracy and pre-emptively defend the way it operates while still acknowledging that the process does not operate meritocratically. These two contradictory narratives can thus be held by candidates simultaneously and mobilised in their narratives to a number of discursive ends, both of which allow individuals to criticise the process without challenging it. While they can and do discuss certain aspects of the process that are not rigorous or meritocratic, this is addressed through other repertoires: for women, it is presented as evidence for their ability to work hard to navigate the appointment process, and in men's accounts, it is justified in meritocratic ways (such as needing directors that are known to the board) or seen as an inevitable part of board diversity initiative that may cease to be a focus when women on boards is not so in the public eye. In all cases, however, any critique of the appointment process is obfuscated or played down.

Notes

1. Public house where alcohol is being sold.
2. An annual list of the 500-largest US industrial corporations, as measured by gross income.

6   Gender and the Pathway to the Boardroom

In this book, we have provided an account of the subjective experiences of aspiring non-executive directors seeking appointments on corporate boards in the UK. The research took place in a climate where the emphasis was on getting more women on boards of directors. We have explored how candidates, both men and women, make sense of the appointment process, how they position themselves as candidates suitable for board roles, how they network to get roles and how they make sense of success and failure. This reveals the presence of gendered discourses in how they make sense of the process, which may contribute to women's difficulty entering the boardroom. It has also revealed how candidates draw on wider social discourses to justify the appointment process, which makes it impervious to critique.

The Right Experience, the Right Personality and the Right Fit

In Chapter 2, we showed how candidates describe the 'ideal' board member and how this discursive construction emerges both explicitly and implicitly throughout the interviews. The ideal board member is constructed around three key aspects: having the right experience, the right personality and the 'fit' with the board. First, the candidates emphasised that boards preferred candidates who have previously held, or currently hold, board roles (Brickley *et al.*, 1999; Fich and White, 2005; Zorn, 2004) or come from certain industry backgrounds. This builds on existing research that suggests that women are not chosen for boards because they do not have the right human capital, as the areas of experience that the ideal has are more commonly held by men. We found that it was a taken-for-granted assumption in candidates' accounts that having the right experience is important for boards and their likelihood of being successful and that the criteria are inflexible and narrow. This belief, therefore, has what we would regard as a 'truth effect' (Gill, 2007), wherein its repetition and common sense nature make it difficult to challenge. It also shows the power of this discourse to dictate who is seen as 'ideal', where those from certain backgrounds—HR, legal and professional services (which tend to have more women in senior roles)—are discursively constructed as not suitable for boards; they have the wrong experience. Where individuals hold what they felt to be functionally identical roles in different industries, such as having been a senior partner in a law firm or an HR director, they describe struggling to translate this experience into the experience they feel boards are looking for. As such, these findings suggest that what is *seen* as the required board experience may be even more restrictive than the literature indicates, as in order to be seen as the 'right' experience, it has to be board-level experience of the *right kind*. It also suggests that those who do 'make it' may have to go through a process of translation to fit their experience into what the boards are looking for and that headhunters have a role in this, as many candidates suggested they had to translate this to headhunters.

We have also highlighted how the ideal board member is constructed as someone with the right personality traits and how these traits are gendered, subjective and individualistic. When describing how they felt they were suited to taking up board roles, candidates frequently emphasised their ability to make high-level strategic decisions and to challenge the board. In women's accounts, this frequently means emphasising traits more commonly associated with masculinity, while traits such as being 'people focused' or risk averse—which have, albeit problematically (Roberts, 2015) been more readily associated with women—were played down. Both men and women from legal backgrounds emphasised needing to demonstrate that they are not risk averse, like 'typical' lawyers (and, perhaps, 'typical' women). The emphasis on having the right personality suggests that the boardroom may operate on norms of masculine and elite models of success, which candidates feel they need to show they fit.

We also outlined that the ideal board member was constructed as someone who is seen to 'fit' with the board, supporting the assertion in the wider literature that board appointments may be biased due to their reliance on subjective criteria and fit, which is often difficult to define (Hill, 1995; Pye, 2000, 2001). We found that individuals frequently emphasised the importance of boards working together, emphasising the importance of fit, in rational or meritocratic terms. What is most problematic when we consider how these discourses are used is that they necessitate and legitimate a focus on subjective criteria under a rational or meritocratic model. This is particularly problematic at the board level because the appointment process is largely based on the chair of the board making the decision, affording them highly subjective decision making regarding aspiring candidates, as observed in other studies (Holgersson, 2013; Wirz, 2014). The emphasis that candidates give to board members needing to have the right personality and fit with the board may explicitly or implicitly justify the appointment process operating on highly subjective criteria and afford it an impression of rationality and/or meritocracy.

Because getting along with the other directors is treated as a vital part of the ability to do the role in candidates' accounts (as we saw in the literature, where 'fit' is seen as a crucial part of the directors' work) (Pye, 2005), judging fitness is described as an essential part of the appointment process.

The reliance on fit and subjective criteria for assessment of candidates is often assumed to make the appointment process more difficult for women or those who do not display similar personal traits to the directors on the board (Meriläinen *et al.*, 2013). Supporting this, this research reveals occurrences where women describe needing to 'perform masculinity' (Mavin and Grandy, 2016a)—for example, by downplaying femininity while also ensuring that they are likeable, physically attractive, polished and groomed (McRobbie, 2009). This co-construction can be seen as a way for them to 'do gender well and differently' (Mavin and Grandy, 2012), while simultaneously performing expressions of femininity and masculinity in their attempts to establish competence (Tienari *et al.*, 2013). The absence of similar discourses in men's accounts suggests that, unlike men, women *need* to perform gender 'correctly', balancing masculine and feminine traits (Kelan, 2010) to be deemed credible.

While in one sense this research supports the human capital explanation for a lack of women on boards (the argument that there simply are not enough women with the senior experience required by boards), we would emphasise the importance of seeing the ideal board member as a form of discursive job description impression management, which has been seen in other research into directors (Westphal, 2010). Westphal argues that directors often characterise their role as 'highly complex, time consuming and demanding, and as requiring either extensive, specialised expertise in a particular area of corporate strategy, extensive general management experience, or both' (Westphal, 2010: p. 321) but that this often does not reflect the reality of the role (ibid., see also Fahlenbrach *et al.*, 2011; Westphal, 1998; Westphal and Khanna, 2003). He concludes that this impression management is a way for directors to enhance the legitimacy of the role and their own status. In this research context, the construction of the ideal board member has both of these consequences: aspiring directors describe the role as requiring specific, rare and elite traits (legitimising the seniority of the role), as well as experience or traits *that they have* (emphasising their own status). This also has the consequence of presenting the appointment process as rational and meritocratic. By emphasising that the ideal board member (who has the right experience, traits and fit with the board) will be chosen, and the rationality behind this construction, an overall impression is given of a meritocratic process: one where directors are chosen according to objective measures of success (Simpson and Kumra, 2016).

This rational and meritocratic perspective of the appointment process is problematic. First, as other researchers have argued, meritocracy is by and large a social construct (Simpson *et al.*, 2010) that has a tendency to obfuscate gender difference (Castilla and Benard, 2010). In the case of directors and how this discourse is mobilised, we find that it results in biased, subjective, masculine and restrictive criteria being rationalised as meritocratic. The backgrounds that are treated as most desired by boards (the 'right' experience) are those that the majority of directors hold (Lowe *et al.*, 2016). This becomes even more problematic when we consider that being recommended or known to the board is a key factor in being appointed and working in the same area or sector leads to networked connections. The preference for the right experience, therefore, also means a preference for candidates *already known to the board through their experience*. The right experience discourse, therefore, acts as a smokescreen as it uses a meritocratic or rational discourse to explain bias towards certain candidates and disguises biases that will inevitably occur in an appointment system that relies largely or solely on recommendations. Similarly, the emphasis placed on the right personality and fit with the board legitimates a subjective appointment process and places it within a meritocratic discourse.

Finally, the requirement that candidates align with the discursive construction of the ideal board member can also be regarded as representing and reproducing norms or socially accepted models of elite recruitment. Other research into the recruitment for elite organisations, such as consultancy firms (Alvesson and Robertson, 2006), executive search firms (Beaverstock *et al.*, 2015) and banking and finance industries (Fisher, 2012), has noted that these are primary sites for the construction of elite identities: the individuals chosen tend to be of high ability (and are told this is what is sought), and the nature of the work is intellectually demanding and often ambiguous (Alvesson and Robertson, 2006). In the case of corporate directors, it could be argued that the emphasis on elite identity markers (the right experience, personality and fit for the boardroom) goes deeper than just presentation of self; it is a way for individuals to demonstrate that they have the right (elite) identity and way of being to be deemed suitable for the board. Elite identification, therefore, has an organisational function: in a day-to-day sense, it helps organisations to control their employees, but it also helps them to recruit, and restrict entry to recruitment, under meritocratic discourses. By constructing and maintaining a successful, credible elite identity, the organisation (or a corporate board) can attract, recruit or retain highly qualified experts (Alvesson and Robertson, 2006).

Strategic Yet Subtle Networking

We also explored aspiring directors' networking practices and how they navigate the board appointment process to gain visibility with board 'gatekeepers' (van den Brink and Benschop, 2014). These findings support the assertion made in the wider literature that aspiring directors see success most commonly (or solely) coming through networking due to the importance of being known to the board. They describe their relationships in highly strategic and instrumental terms, presenting networking as 'work' or 'labour', with the overall aim of collecting as many connections as possible. That we found this was evident for men and women challenges the notion that women have functionally different networks or networking practices than men or that they favour affective or 'strong' ties (Granovetter, 1973; Ibarra, 1993); rather, all the aspiring directors we spoke to suggest through their narratives that they seek to connect with as many individuals as they can, with the primary aim of gaining visibility. While candidates describe highly strategic networking practices, this is upheld alongside an insistence that networking must be done subtly (in the right way) and that they appear not to be pushing 'too hard', as this will be detrimental to their success. This again highlights the importance of understanding networking as a practice that has to be done in the right way, not as something abstract that is done or finished at the point the connection is made.

The concern with networking in the 'right' way is mobilised in two ways: first, it emerged when candidates implied that their networking needed to appear to be subtle to people they were 'targeting' and second in how the language used in the research interviews gave the impression that while they are being strategic, they are also, simultaneously and paradoxically, not 'really' networking hard. We found this particularly in the interviews when they explained subtle networking as an individual preference, personality or previous career success, presenting the decision as a choice they have individually made rather than one which is required in order to be successful. This manifests in the research interview, then, as them being 'subtle' about being 'subtle' in their networking, which has the effect of acting as a smokescreen or obfuscation of how the process operates. Rather than challenging the need to be subtle, they state that it is a personal preference or decision that makes this choice individual rather than a systemic issue.

The requirement for subtlety makes more sense when we compare it to other areas of elite recruitment, which are frequently categorised by social norms that emphasise the individual being sought out or found by the recruiter or headhunter rather than putting themselves forward (Alvesson and Robertson, 2006; Beaverstock *et al.*, 2015; Fisher, 2012). In this context, by emphasising their need, choice and/or ability to be subtle in their networking practices, candidates emphasise their elite status. This can be regarded as a kind of impression management, which results in the justification of the system operating as it is; in this case, it gives the impression that there is nothing inherently problematic with the need to be found: it is just a process that candidates have to work around. This highlights, as van den Brink and Benschop (2014) argue, the importance of conducting research that examines individuals' networking practices and how they describe them rather than just examining outcomes.

From a gendered perspective, men's and women's accounts of their networking practices are remarkably similar: both emphasise the need to be both strategic and subtle, and both see networking as a way to strategically gain visibility. We see the most significant gendered difference when we look at how they explain these practices and how they navigate the need to be simultaneously strategic yet subtle in their networking. While men described not wanting to push too hard by stating it was best for them or best for gaining success, women more commonly sought to avoid appearing too 'desperate' or 'pushy', and using gendered, feminised and, at times, sexualised language—most notably one woman making reference to standing on a street corner. Their descriptions of strategic networking also present a dilemma when we look at it longitudinally because they are required to be constantly (net)working in order to be successful. This was evident in later interviews where they described networking in order to work at being visible. Often, this was justified by stating that headhunters or chairs having 'front of mind' bias, where they would only remember or put forward individuals they had seen recently and, therefore, requiring candidates to (subtly) keep visible. This also highlights the value in conducting longitudinal research, as while in the first interviews all candidates described strategic networking to gain visibility, the process of *maintaining* visibility was more complex and made the subtlety more difficult to uphold. Often, the study of networks and networking can treat them as static states (an individual is either visible or not, in the network or not) rather than treating networking, and the visibility it affords, as a constant doing or practice (van den Brink and Benschop, 2009).

We also highlighted the importance of recommendations or sponsorship for gaining NED roles: candidates emphasised the need to be recommended by others, put forward by a headhunter or recommended by another director to a headhunter, appointing board or chair. While the wider literature on networks and progression has highlighted the importance of (particularly women) having sponsors in the workplace (Ibarra *et al.*, 2010), in the case of directors, this can be theorised as a form of co-sponsorship or peer sponsorship, as often the person sponsoring them was not someone necessarily more senior. In this case, we see individuals who are at similar or indiscernible levels of seniority putting each other forward for roles; the power they have is already being visible to the gatekeeper. This suggests a need to broaden understanding of how sponsorship may operate at very senior levels of organisations and in elite networks. While being a sponsor necessitates the individual holding a position of relative power that s/he is able to leverage, in director networks, the notion of 'power' is bound up in having access to current board members or gatekeepers, which does not necessarily align with traditional hierarchies. In this area, individuals can sponsor each other, as they may have access to differing networks and boards.

The importance of being recommended for roles was present across candidates' accounts; however, women discussed this more commonly than men, particularly through needing to build connections with other women and put each other forward for roles as a way to tackle the historical Old Boys' networks. Women here take for granted that they will face a barrier due to their networks being in their relative infancy compared with men's and, therefore, have to develop strategies to tackle it. Their approach chimes with a neoliberal feminist perspective, where women's disadvantage is taken for granted, and they work to build individual or group solutions to overcome it rather than, for instance, mobilising together to challenge the *status quo*. Their solution instead is to play the men 'at their own game' (Rottenberg, 2014), accepting 'work' as their responsibility to engender their own success by surmounting barriers. It is also interesting to note how women's networking is divided on gendered lines: they engage in heterophily when individually targeting gatekeepers (who are most commonly men), as well as building connections with women both individually and at women's networks or events.

The strategies women have for their networking practices are again challenged, however, when we examine how they discuss formal networks. Particularly, later in the research—on their second or third interviews—many of the women outright rejected women's networks, regarding them as being a waste of time because of their focus on 'talk' rather than action (Bierema, 2005) and the absence of men. By comparison, men rarely discussed using formal networks. On the few occasions when women discussed attending or joining networks that are not focused on women (there was one, for instance, aimed at getting lawyers on boards), they criticised these for being populated only by older men and, therefore, reproducing a kind of Old Boys' network. This is a concern, as it suggests that formal NED networks may have the effect of ghettoising and reaffirming gender segregation, creating highly gendered spaces that are generally not regarded as supporting individuals' chances of success. It may also suggest that in areas where there is emphasis on informal, one-to-one networking, formal networks have little capacity to tackle gender bias.

Talking About *Leaning in* and *Sitting Back*

Finally, we have outlined the wider social discourses that candidates use to make sense of the process overall and particularly how they explain their success and failure. This highlights the existence of two contrasting discourses for making sense of the process overall and reveals how men's and women's adoption of these sense-making discourses is gendered. Women's accounts of their success and failure draw on a 'lean-in' discourse; they attribute their success to their ability to lean in and push for roles, particularly through networking. This is often in contradiction to their insistence that we discussed in Chapter 4 that they must not be 'too pushy' in their networking. This contradiction can be explained as a difference between present sense making and hindsight: when they are successful, they are afforded the ability to retrospectively make sense of networking as work that was necessary in order to get roles. When accounting for their failure to get a board role in the research period, they similarly related it to their work and their actions, internalising reasons for their failure and attributing it to not networking hard enough. By doing so, the only solution they provide for themselves is to network harder and push for roles (while all the while ensuring that they are not being *too* pushy).

In contrast to women's sense making, men's accounts drew on a 'sitting-back' discourse. When retrospectively accounting for their success in gaining roles, they emphasised the informal nature of the process, the relatively little 'work' they had to do to be chosen and how they were approached for roles by headhunters or chairs rather than approaching them. This sense making draws again on norms of elite recruitment, and this is further seen in how they emphasised markers of their elite status, the elite spaces these interactions occurred within and the highly informal nature of the process. When discussing their failure to be appointed over the research period, men tended to relate it to their decision to 'sit back', attributing it to a personal decision to be choosy when selecting a board role (again, emphasising their elite status and ability to be choosy) or a need to be patient and wait until the focus on women had died down. These failure discourses, therefore, *externalise* failure in their insistence that it is due to factors out of their control or internalise it only so much that it is attributed to their decision (not their inability) to network well or not being suitable for board roles.

The combination and contradiction between the lean-in/sit-back discourses and the strategic/subtle networking discussed earlier also represent a wider paradox or double-bind occurring in the case of women on boards, where we see women adopting the active and deliberate work advocated by the *Lean In* rhetoric and applying it to director appointments. The norms of recruitment and identity work so that we see emerging in this their accounts and how they reference markers of elite status (for instance, the insistence that individuals must be subtle, patient and wait to be found) challenges ideas of leaning in that advocate women being confident and tackling internal barriers to push forward for their success. Criticisms of *Lean In* (Foster, 2016; Rottenberg, 2014, 2018) or 'confidence cult(ure)' (Gill and Orgad, 2016) have drawn attention to its privileged perspective; the lean-in rhetoric is a particular kind of feminism that is only available to a particular kind of woman and role due to its tendency to fail to fully account for structural barriers women may face (Foster, 2015). However, this research raises another criticism: that leaning in can also be incongruent with success, even for those already in elite or privileged positions. We found throughout this research that the norms of appointments at the board level in the UK are based (still) on norms of gentlemanly capitalism (Augar, 2008), where success comes from 'sitting back' and being found and that pushing forward too much could be detrimental to success. The lean-in rhetoric may, therefore, be detrimental to women's progression, not because these women are not senior enough, held back by structural issues (cf. Gill and Orgad, 2016) or because they are holding themselves back with internal self-barriers (Sandberg, 2013) but because of the world they are operating in. Given that the many examples of corporate feminism rhetoric are almost exclusively American (see Gill and Orgad, 2016), they may also be part of a very specific kind of American success narrative, which is at odds with how British business elites operate.

We heard a great deal in this research an *easier for women* discourse, or in the words of one male interviewee, there has 'never been a better time to be a woman'. For women, this emerged as an implicit or explicit statement that it was easier than *it had ever been* for women to get roles and formed part of their motivation for seeking roles—it was a good opportunity for them to start looking now, given that boards were under pressure to appoint women or address their gender balance. This discourse emerged most frequently in men's sense making, however, with an insistence that it is easier for women *than men* to get roles and that if they (the men) had been women, they would have found it easier.

The way that men used this idea to account for their failure (and indeed even men who had been successful asserted the same belief) is notable for a number of reasons. First, over the course of the research period, only 30% of new FTSE 350 board roles went to women (Brown *et al.*, 2015). Although this is a rise from the average 10% in the period before the target was set, it suggests that the bias towards women is overstated; at the least, it suggests that when men are unsuccessful, they are in competition with other men far more commonly than with women. Despite this, no men in the research discussed feeling in competition with other men or other men's success as contributing to their failure. Men primarily attribute failure to the presumed increase in women seeking roles, suggesting that the women-on-boards agenda provides a narrative within which men can make sense of failure without challenging the notion that they will be successful. Again, it is notable that while women drew on the women-on-boards target as motivation for seeking roles, they rarely used it to make sense of failure: no woman thought that the problem was an overrepresentation of other women (or men) seeking roles, and there was also little competitiveness between women.

The easier for women discourse is also notable because, when it formed part of individuals' sense making, it was related solely to the

Davies' review and women-on-boards targets rather than a preference for women because they are more desirable candidates, better for business or necessary as a way to address social injustice. Both the business case and the social justice case for women on boards (Seierstad, 2016) were conspicuously absent; the advantage for women is solely attributed to the need to meet the target. While the business-focused target approach was likely useful for gaining traction with UK business audiences (Sealy *et al.*, 2017), the business case was not ultimately part of candidates' narratives. While individuated justice or meritocratic discourses were evident—a belief that women are an 'untapped pool' of qualified talent— the belief that women and diversity are valuable additions to boards was notably absent. This could be interpreted as a backlash against the target: women being regarded as 'tokens' who are there solely to fulfil a quota (Shilton *et al.*, 2010), men feeling they are at a disadvantage due to 'positive discrimination' in favour of women and it being presumed that the quality of boards has decreased as a result (Ahern and Dittmar, 2012; Shilton *et al.*, 2010). This suggests then that the Davies' review had similar effects and backlash often attributed to quotas, despite it being a voluntary target. This finding chimes with Seierstad's (2016) assertion that in cases where quotas or targets are utilised, it is important to examine their effects beyond just an increase in women. In this case, we were able to pinpoint a strong set of discourses that followed the voluntary approach to women on boards that the UK took. Yet those discourses are strikingly similar to the discourses mobilised in the wake of quotas (Humbert *et al.*, 2019).

The strength of this discourse may also be indicative of evidence of interviewees treating the research interviews as an opportunity to challenge the women-on-boards initiative. Given that academics were (seen as) key actors in the women-on-boards agenda in the UK (Seierstad *et al.*, 2017) and that this research was connected with a headhunter known for being committed to women on boards, interviewees may have aligned it with the overall women-on-boards initiative and used the interview as an opportunity to challenge the assertion that women face a barrier and state instead that men now face a disadvantage. As has also been found in much gender research (Kelan, 2014; Gill, 2007; Scharff, 2012), men often expressed criticisms of gender equality agendas as 'disclaimers' (Gill, 1993; Hewitt and Stokes, 1975). In this context, they are positive about the need to get women on boards; they are well versed on the subject of diversity (cf. Kelan, 2014) and insist that the change is positive while also being highly critical or presenting sexist accounts.

Precarious Privilege

When examining the board appointment process through the experiences of aspiring directors, these research findings should also be placed within a number of wider social contexts. First, we must locate directors as part of the corporate elite, a group that is known to be exclusionary to outsiders and particularly effective at reproducing itself. Second, this research can contribute to our understanding of how women's experiences of being in this elite are gendered. Third, we can use these findings to examine how the women-on-boards agenda has affected board appointments, if at all.

Corporate directors in the FTSE 350 and indeed many of the interviewees in this research can be understood as members of the corporate 'wealth elite' or 'professional executive class' (Bennett *et al.*, 2009; Savage *et al.*, 2013). This has been outlined by researchers into class (Savage *et al.*, 2013), which, through large-scale sociological, research points to the existence of an emergent kind of elite class that is culturally different from historical power elites and occupies a unique space in class and society in the UK (ibid.). This research gives some insight into how members of this class make sense of their existence and how they legitimise elite recruitment.

Throughout the research, we found a tendency for aspiring directors—and later those who are appointed—to both explicitly and implicitly advocate for the process operating as it does. In some cases, this emerges implicitly: very few candidates actively criticised the appointment process, possibly because they felt they had little control over it or the capability to change it, and as such just accepted it as taken for granted. Interviewees' accounts contained numerous examples of how they have learned how to 'play the game' through focusing on strategic and subtle networking, understanding how search practice operates and how they can use it to their advantage or through emphasising how their experience translates into the 'right' experience or working to demonstrate how they 'fit' with the board. Where we do see criticism of the system, it is frequently couched in these highly individualistic terms rather than advocating broader changes.

In some cases, justification for the board appointment process came through more explicitly through people stating that it is necessary for the appointment process to operate as it does. For instance, many described how the recruitment process involving recommendations and connections with other individuals allows boards to ensure that the people they appoint are trustworthy. Similarly, we found candidates stating that directors need to fit the board in order to be good directors, where the board is conceptualised as a unit, and 'fit' is a necessary part of their role. This belief, therefore, justifies a highly subjective, restrictive and elitist appointment process on meritocratic grounds.

Criticism of the appointment process was also restricted by candidates' tendency to draw on individualised discourses when discussing how they navigate it. In the case of networking, it was taken for granted that networking is the only route to get roles but that it had to be done subtly.

This was often described in highly individualised terms: they would assert that this method was best for them; they network subtly because they feel uncomfortable being pushy, for instance, or they have achieved success so far by having 'never been a planner'. Similarly, when retrospectively accounting for success, this would be attributed to personal decisions and actions—having networked in the right way or with the right people or having the right experience. When accounting for failure, this would be aligned with not having networked enough (women) or being choosy and patient (men). In all cases, this underlying discourse of self-responsibility and individualism reaffirms the notion that they have to work hard to overcome the system as it stands rather than challenging the status quo. This is also seen in the meritocratic discursive effects of the ideal board member discourse: emphasis on the right experience and traits supports a notion that the process is rational, meritocratic and rigorous.

Overall, these findings suggest that while this new financial elite are characterised by a presumed opening up of their recruitment processes (McDowell, 1997), particularly with the increased appointment of women and people outside the traditional Old Boys' networks, the way that directors are appointed is remarkably resilient to change. It suggests a space within which new cultural norms are re-enacted and offers insight into how these cultural norms and discourses are upheld within this wealth elite. The findings from this research suggest that corporate directors may be theorised as sitting at an intersection between being part of the 'new' capitalism and a bastion of the old norms of gentlemanly capitalism (Augar, 2008). It is new in the sense that it is ambiguous and non-hierarchical, unlike executive director roles, non-executive directors do not sit at the top of a hierarchy with clear steps for progression. Instead, candidates gain roles by moving laterally, which they discursively cast as moving up. On the other hand, the very existence of corporate boards of directors is historic and harks back to norms of business that focus on trust between individuals, Old Boys' networks and restricting access, which are still embedded within the appointment process. This allows the discourses that surround this particular world to be made up of both cultures: the process of appointment is simultaneously highly rational (they need very specific kinds of people who are appointed rigorously and meritocratically) and highly irrational and informal (they need people they like and trust).

We should also locate this research into women on boards by considering it in relation to other research into women in elite roles (Mavin and Grandy, 2016a, 2016b) and the increased presence of women in this corporate elite. The research provides a case study of a particular subsection of a population, an organisation (theoretically rather than geographically) that has in recent years seen a rapid increase in the number of women, and it, therefore, offers insight into this particular elite of women, their experiences and how they make sense of their position.

Building on Savage and colleagues' (2013) assertion that class can be used to strategically open up areas of concern, we argue that in the case of women on boards, gender must also be used as a way to strategically open up areas of concern, to move beyond body counting and to understand how their experiences can illuminate the corporate elite. These women are in a unique space that offers new avenues for theorisation, as the board appointment process can be regarded as a site within which to examine how their privilege is conferred, contested and defended (Mavin and Grandy, 2016b). Women in this position hold power and have made it through the 'glass ceiling'; however, they are also marginalised (Mavin and Grandy, 2016b). Studying their experiences of seeking to move (or moving) from one privileged space to another, as is the case when seeking a new role, can offer an understanding of how gender is embedded in these spaces, how women negotiate their privilege and disadvantage and what discourses are navigated and upheld in the process.

Because they are simultaneously privileged and abject, women in this corporate elite have to work, both literally and discursively, to hold on to that privilege, in a way that is seen much less significantly in men's accounts. Similar accounts are found in ethnographic work into women who occupy minority spaces in highly masculinised spaces, such as in banking and finance industries (Fisher, 2012; McDowell, 1997), where they have to work to establish credibility and legitimacy. This also contributes to their discourses around meritocracy; their insistence that they have or will achieve success through their hard work and their own ability is part of the discursive work they have to do in order to uphold the notion that they were or will be appointed meritocratically (Kelan, 2010). This may also contribute to the difference in discourses used by men and women in how they make sense of networking and the process overall; women's starkly neoliberal discourses that emphasised the work they put in were mobilised to argue that they achieved success through hard work rather than nepotism or bias towards women due to the quota. In comparison, men's discourses that emphasised the relatively little work they put into networking and the informality of the process are not available to women, as this would challenge the notion of meritocracy that their privilege is based on. This places women in a double-bind: when they are not successful in gaining roles, they insist that they have to work harder, and when they are successful, they have to subscribe to the process operating as it does because it is the system that led to their success.

While women in senior roles still remain in a relative minority, the (rapid) increase in the number of women on boards also allows us to examine how their experiences are influenced by gender, how they do gender well and differently and how women's relationships and interactions with each other are played out in the board appointment process. One notable gendered discourse that emerges throughout the research relates to Mavin and Grandy's (2016a, 2016b) work on respectable business femininity: '[a] discursive and relational process that explains the tensions women elite leaders can experience at the nexus of being sometimes privileged, embedded notions of embodied leadership as masculine, and wider expectations of acceptable embodied femininity' (Mavin and Grandy, 2016b: p. 380). As in Mavin and Grandy's work, women seeking roles have these tensions manifest in the way they discuss a need to discipline their bodies and bring them into line with respectable business femininity, such as through not having pink nails, straightening curly hair or wearing appropriate clothing so as not to be rejected by a business-conservative boardroom. These findings support the notion that women may be excluded from the boardroom for their femininity not 'fitting' a masculine model of success or at least that women note this incompatibility and work around the expectations.

Femininity was also treated negatively throughout in the repetition of negative connotations attached to it. Women in this study frequently used exaggerated feminine terms to refer to negative aspects of the process: women who network too hard are 'shameless' or prostitutes; self-limiting doubts are described as 'female doubts'; they are concerned with being too 'desperate' or 'pushy'; women's networks are 'handbag clubs', et cetera. This can be seen as a form of negative intra-gender relations (Mavin and Grandy, 2012) through its negative description of other women in the space, but it also operates as a way for women to distance themselves from other women, particularly those who they do not see as being as successful or as likely to succeed as they are. This kind of Queen Bee syndrome (ibid.) or tendency to be negative about other women becomes even more significant in the board space because the hierarchies are difficult to navigate, and there are no clear paths to progression. This also results in a contradictory discourse wherein women emphasise the importance of their working with other women to be successful, particularly in the oft-repeated assertion that there is a special place in hell for women who do not help other women. We see throughout their accounts then a kind of gendered elite sense making; in the process of criticising other women, they are emphasising their elite status and using gendered language to do so.

As noted earlier in relation to women's sense making, there is also an incompatibility between the model of success often advocated by the *Lean In* rhetoric and the norms of what is acceptable in the elite's appointment process. As well as being problematic due to it not necessarily leading to success, the strength of the neoliberal feminism discourses also results in the process being justified; by emphasising how their hard work led to success, women maintain the perspective that they worked hard to get the roles, even while success is connected to being known by and to the right people. This is also seen in the way that they discursively draw parallels between their experiences of seeking board roles and other areas of recruitment; this normalises the appointment process, and thus obfuscates some of the barriers that are specifically related to elite recruitment—namely, the lack of public advertisement for board roles and the reliance on executive search firms and networking. They also have to work harder to uphold their privilege in this contested position (Atewologun and Sealy, 2014) given the strength of the 'easier for women' discourse. This backlash, with the underlying message that women who do not 'deserve' roles may be appointed, may require women to work even harder to discursively emphasise meritocracy, even within a biased appointment process.

New Horizons for the Field of Women on Boards

The findings from this research have a number of key contributions to the field of gender and organisations. First, we offer a contribution to the extant research on women on boards. The data presented has highlighted key aspects of what is deemed to constitute an ideal board member, showing that candidates' conception of the ideal board member is restrictive and gendered, and it narrows entry through a reliance on having the right experience, the right personality and the right fit with the board. This draws on and develops the debates in the literature around the human capital of directors, showing how directors adopt human capital explanations in their sense making. Future research could develop this further by examining how this ideal is conceptualised by those who sit on boards to understand if it is a repertoire adopted during the appointment process or if it is also part of being a director and if the conception is similar for those who have been successful. Westphal (2010) has highlighted this job role 'impression management' occurring in existing directors in the US, but it would develop our understanding further to examine this in the UK context and, particularly, in relation to the effect of the women-on-boards target.

The same research development could be applied to the concept of 'fit'. This research offers empirical support for a reliance on fit as part of the appointment process, something that has been often cited in criticisms of the board appointment process (see, for example, Doldor *et al.*, 2016) but that is less often empirically demonstrated or sufficiently operationalised. It is also, problematically, often assumed to be necessary for an effective board: this study and others (Pye, 2001) have shown that it is regarded as an important part of a director's role and, therefore, not incongruous with notions of merit. Given its persistence and the impossibility in defining or measuring it, future research in this area could examine if and how 'fit' occurs within the boardroom setting and how directors' interactional norms are defined within boardroom conversations. This would provide empirical evidence for or against the existence of 'fit' and thereby challenge or confirm its importance in recruitment practices. This is an area where adopting discursive or conversation analysis of boardroom conversations, for example, could add significant value to better understand how fit is enacted and embodied by directors.

This book also contributes to the women-on-boards debates and corporate governance literature by offering an understanding of how the board appointment process operates. While the reliance on networks has been identified in other research too, this study also supports the social capital explanation for a lack of women on boards, but places it in a wider context. It demonstrates the implications of this network-based recruitment in elites that it required individuals to be both strategic and subtle in their networking practices. This research contributes to wider theoretical work on networks and networking through demonstrating the importance of taking a networking practices approach rather than a networks approach (van den Brink and Benschop, 2009), as it reveals the work that goes into establishing and maintaining networks and how this work is gendered. The notion of subtle networking has not been identified in other literatures and is worthy of further examination.

This research also responds to calls in the literature for research into women in senior elite roles (Mavin and Grandy, 2014) and in doing so contributes both to the literature on gender and organisations and gender and elites. Recruitment for a specific, high-status role offers insight into barriers these women face, even having 'made it' through the glass ceiling, and the work they undertake against negotiate privilege and disadvantage (Sealy, 2010) and thus offers a site for theory development in relation to gender and organisations. It has shown areas where they face similar challenges to those women lower down in organisations— such as needing to ensure that their appearance is in line with business femininity—but it also illuminates what is unique to their privileged position and is specific to their seeking new roles within UK boardrooms. While women articulated having to balance a masculine model of success while ensuring that they are feminine, polished and groomed, these notions of success relate to both gender and class: being 'polished' is a display of femininity more available to those from higher socio-economic backgrounds (Brown, 2016; Witz *et al.,* 2003) and is attributed to the 'conservative' nature of boardrooms. This research sought to contribute to our understanding of how women negotiate their positions in and out of privilege and disadvantage and in doing so supports Mavin and Grandy's assertion that women in these roles must do 'gender well and differently' (Mavin and Grandy, 2012) in order to uphold credibility. More broadly, it demonstrates the importance of moving beyond a 'body counting' starting point to gender equality by highlighting the gendered practices at work in the appointment process, even while numerically the number of women has increased.

Finally, the research also contributes to knowledge on the existence and reproduction of a corporate elite. Throughout the research, candidates' accounts were imbued with elite discourses, references to indicators of elite status and descriptions of elite networking and recruitment practices. Paradoxically, in some cases, they were also imbued with discourses of meritocracy. As in Seierstad's (2016) research into women who were appointed after the quota was brought forward in Norway, issues of merit and gender are implicated in individuals' arguments and accounts and often in contradictory ways. In this research, we see how meritocracy is fundamental to notions of what makes the ideal board member and can, therefore, act as a smokescreen for bias: it is argued that those with the right experience will be appointed, while having the 'right' experience also means being in the same networks as current directors. Understanding directors as members of a corporate elite makes this emphasis on meritocratic discourses theoretically interesting, as meritocracy may be a way that they justify their location within elites, particularly when it is discursively combined with references to their elite status. This also suggests that those involved in the process either explicitly or implicitly justify the process operating as it does. Either this occurs on meritocratic terms through advocating the importance of getting people who can be trusted or on individualised terms where discourses of self-responsibility and self-blame are used to explain outcomes of the process. This may suggest that meritocracy is part of the 'culture of being' (Savage *et al.*, 2013) that this elite group operates by, contributing to our understanding of elites and suggesting an area for further research.

There's Never Been a Better Time to Be a Woman?

It is important to place this research within the social context and the influence of the women-on-boards agenda in the UK to better understand its policy implications. The increase of women directors between 2011 and 2015[1] (from 12.5% to 25% in the FTSE 100) was regarded as a success (Sealy *et al.*, 2017). The final report (Davies, 2015) contained a number of highly positive quotes praising Lord Davies and the campaign for their immense achievement. From a body-counting perspective, the Davies' review and target was an accomplishment; however, there was, throughout the process and time period, very little (space for) critical feminist engagement with the women-on-boards phenomena. This research has attempted to start this critical engagement by highlighting the problems and potential backlash with the unquestioned narrative of progress. This research, like Seierstad's (2016), highlights the importance of examining how men and women are affected by the existence of a target or quota beyond just the numerical increase of women on boards.

As the academics who worked on this initiative acknowledge themselves, the success of the gender target in the UK depended on gaining broad support from businesses and different political parties and governments, and it, therefore, needed to have broad political appeal (Sealy *et al.*, 2017). They argue that this resulted in the initiative having to avoid adopting radical, social justice arguments and instead draw on pseudo-business logics so as to avoid alienating corporate audiences. Although this is understandable in relation to engendering social change, the lack of critical feminist or radical analyses may contribute to a progress narrative being adopted without assessment of the wider implications beyond an increase of women. This critical analysis is important first because despite the 'problem' of a lack of women on boards being associated with an opaque system, the increased number of women is not necessarily indicative of change in the process itself. Second, there is evidence of a backlash in the now taken-for-granted assumption that there has never been a better time to be a woman and that men now face a disadvantage.

One of the problems with the way that the women-on-boards agenda has occurred in the UK is that it has taken a body counting, gender and organisation perspective (Calás *et al.*, 2014): the problem of the 'lack of women' was identified, a target of 25% women on boards was set, with a deadline, and the target was met. Particularly, given that the speed with which the target was achieved, having been set in 2011 and was then reached in 2015, suggests that the Davies' review and focus on getting women onto boards has operated as a discursive quota: while there was no threat of legal action, the outcomes (both positive and negative) were the same. The increased number of women has also elicited negative responses in the form of a backlash (Humbert *et al.*, 2019).

The way that this discourse is mobilised by candidates emphasises how the women on boards initiative may be seen as occurring in a very specific time period, even by those going through it. For women, they need to 'use this window' of opportunity to seek roles at a time when boards are required (as per the target) to address the scarcity of women on boards. For men, it emerges as a need for them to bide their time or be patient (i.e. wait for this window to close) at which point it is assumed they will be more likely to be successful. Given that these discourses are tied to a short-term view of the target and agenda rather than discussed as a sea change, challenges the notion that the rapid increase is indicative of sustained and long-lasting change. Similarly, women's use of the easier-for-women discourse, alongside a reluctance or inability to challenge the process and reliance on meritocratic discourses, makes the process further impervious to critique, because there has 'never been a better time to be a woman', they cannot challenge the process that has led to their success. The fact that those who are currently seeking roles (or have succeeded in being appointed) describe this as a window or phase in history suggests, even more problematically, that there is little evidence of long-term change in attitudes towards women or a broader range of candidates being appointed. It is problematic that even women who have been successful do not describe the focus on women directors as anything other than relating to the target or as a short-term change.

While this research highlights the lack of a social justice case for women on boards in individuals' accounts (Seierstad and colleagues [2017] have commented in relation to the UK too), it also questions the success of the business case. The business case for women on boards, which was such a part of the public discussion in the UK, is notably and surprisingly absent; instead, there is an active and perceptible focus on appointing women as a way to meet the Davies' target. The business case is also not embedded in individuals' accounts and is not a discursive repertoire available to aspiring directors; women seeking board roles are not describing accounts of pushing themselves forward for roles on account of their gender. When they do account for their success on the basis of being a woman, it is often done apologetically, as it goes against discourses of meritocracy that they are more insistent on maintaining. While the business case might be useful for persuading boards that they should be choosing women (and it is beyond the scope of this research to assess the level to which this occurs), it is not useful for individuals as they are going through the process due to its incompatibility with meritocracy and the norms of elite reproduction. This has policy implications, as it suggests the value of using a business case to advocate for gender equality may be limited in its success if they are not becoming part of the rhetoric around appointing women.

We align, therefore, with Seierstad and colleagues' assertion (2017) that in the UK context, the political action to increase the number of women on boards was largely due to a need to respond to other global legislative changes but will not necessarily result in actors, politicians, businesses and boards (or even directors themselves) buying into the idea that appointing women will be good from either a business or a social justice perspective (Seierstad *et al.*, 2017). It also aligns with Doldor and colleagues' (2016) assertion that discussions around diversity need to move beyond a social justice versus business case argument in order to better understand how organisations, actors and governments may be encouraged to engage in diversity changes for different reasons. The force of the 'voluntary' nature of the Davies review instead made it business *critical* that organisations engage: search firms as a way to respond to a growth in the market and boards to protect their reputation from being 'named and shamed' (Davies, 2011). This raises challenges for moving the women-on-boards agenda forward, however, if the success is related to reluctance rather than commitment to change.

We have noted throughout this book that women on boards as a topic for study has often been ghettoised, insomuch as it has not been readily addressed by gender and organisation scholars or critical feminist research, nor is it often considered as part of the work of organisational diversity practitioners. This, we would argue, is to the detriment of critical engagement with what boards represent. Much academic work on women on boards in the UK has been dominated by a relatively small number of academics within or connected to the corporate world, which has been instrumental in driving the women-on-boards agenda forward; however, it makes it less possible for them to critique the elite they are examining. We find this throughout the political engagement too, wherein those individuals and organisations that have been involved most heavily (politicians, businesses, boards, chairs, executive search firms, elite corporations and academics) are largely members of the corporate elite themselves or want to gain access to this elite. The concentration of these same individuals examining the process afforded them the ability to set the parameters for the problem and the solution, with no specific mandate (or motivation) to change the process itself (cf. Doldor *et al.*, 2016).[2] While the outcomes in terms of the number of women gaining roles has been positive, it has maintained power in a small, narrow elite of directors, headhunters and academics, resulting in an unavoidable and uncritical progress narrative which further academic research should problematise. This underlines the need for more critical research (for an example, see Clarke [2019]). It also opens up new questions, such as asking if women on boards start changing the conversation on gender equality in the organisation more widely (see, for example, Kirsch and Sauerborn, 2019).

This is not to say that there has been no change in how directors are appointed or that the increased number of women on boards in the UK should be treated entirely problematically. The increased focus on getting women onto boards has engendered a great deal of wider discussion around the role of women in corporate boards, and the reports following 2015 have emphasised the need to focus on the executive pipeline, which may encourage a reinvigoration of research into gender and organisations and the barriers to women's progression at senior levels. It has also opened up the possibility of their study, and we have shown in this book that the field is ripe for more critical approaches. The research is inevitably routed in a specific historic and social context and took place when there was a peak interest in women on boards in the UK. However, since then, the agenda has moved on to focus on the gender pay gap, #MeToo and the overshadowing Brexit. This book has suggested that while women increasingly gain seats at the boardroom table, the journey to the boardroom continues to be gendered.

Notes

1. Lord Davies ceased to lead the women-on-boards agenda in 2015; however, it was taken on by other leaders. The year 2015 marked the end of his leadership of the process.
2. As a demonstration of this, in addition to a number of the candidates being connected to each other (even when they were not recruited through the same channels), 5 of the 30 candidates described a personal connection with Lord Davies, and three of these noted how being connected with him had been beneficial to their chances of getting a board role.

Appendices

Transcription Notations

The form of transcription used in this book is verbatim text and includes some aspects of Jefferson transcription listed next.

Punctuation is used throughout quotes from interviews in order to add clarity. Most commonly we have added commas (,) question marks (?) colons (:) and semi-colons (;) where necessary grammatically to add clarity to the text.

-is used to denote occasions where the speaker ends a sentence or word abruptly but without pausing.

[ ] Words inside square brackets we have added for clarification, or in replacement of words that have been redacted to protect anonymity of the interviewees.

(. . .) denotes redacted text.

(.) micro pause; a notable pause of no significant length.

(0.2) a number inside brackets denotes a timed pause (0.2 = 2 seconds). This is a pause long enough to time and subsequently show in transcription.

^ ^ These symbols around text demonstrate the text was spoken more softly than the person's usual speech

CAPITALS where capital letters appear it denotes that something was said loudly or shouted

" " talk in speech marks was used where the interviewee is quoting someone else

hehe or HEHE denotes laughter or loud laughter

= denotes latched speech or a continuation of talk.

References

Acker, J. (1990). Hierarchies, jobs, bodies: A theory of gendered organizations. *Gender & Society*, 4(2), 139–158.

Acker, J. (1992). From sex roles to gendered institutions. *Contemporary Sociology: A Journal of Reviews*, 21(5), 565–569.

Adams, R. B. (2016). Women on boards: The superheroes of tomorrow? *Leadership Quarterly*, 27(3), 371–386.

Adams, R. B., Hermalin, B. E., & Weisbach, M. S. (2010). The role of boards of directors in corporate governance: A conceptual framework and survey. *Journal of Economic Literature*, 48(1), 58–107.

Adams, S. M., & Flynn, P. M. (2005). Local knowledge advances women's access to corporate boards. *Corporate Governance: An International Review*, 13(6), 836–846.

Adamson, M., & Kelan, E. K. (2019). "Female Heroes": Celebrity executives as postfeminist role models. *British Journal of Management*, 30(4), 981–996.

Ahern, K. R., & Dittmar, A. K. (2012). The changing of the boards: The impact on firm valuation of mandated female board representation. *The Quarterly Journal of Economics*, 127(1), 137–197.

Albright, M. (2016). Op ed—Madeleine Albright: My undiplomatic moment. *New York Times*. Retrieved from: www.nytimes.com/2016/02/13/opinion/madeleine-albright-my-undiplomatic-moment.html. March 12, 2019.

Aluchna, M., & Aras, G. (2018). *Women on corporate boards: An international perspective*. New York: Routledge.

Alvesson, M., & Robertson, M. (2006). The best and the brightest: The construction, significance and effects of elite identities in consulting firms. *Organization*, 13(2), 195–224.

Arfken, D. E., Bellar, S. L., & Helms, M. M. (2004). The ultimate glass ceiling revisited: The presence of women on corporate boards. *Journal of Business Ethics*, 50(2), 177–186.

Atewologun, D., & Sealy, R. (2014). Experiencing privilege at ethnic, gender and senior intersections. *Journal of Managerial Psychology*, 29(4), 423–439.

Augar, P. (2008). *The death of gentlemanly capitalism: The rise and fall of London's investment banks*. London: Penguin.

Bear, S., Rahman, N., & Post, C. (2010). The impact of board diversity and gender composition on corporate social responsibility and firm reputation. *Journal of Business Ethics*, 97(2), 207–221.

Beaverstock, J. V., Faulconbridge, J. R., & Hall, S. J. E. (2015). *The globalization of executive search: Professional services strategy and dynamics in the contemporary world.* London: Routledge.

Becker, G. S. (1964). *Human capital: A theoretical and empirical analysis.* London: Routledge.

Bennett, T., Savage, M., Silva, E. B., Warde, A., Gayo-Cal, M., & Wright, D. (2009). *Culture, class, distinction.* London: Routledge.

Benschop, Y. (2009). The micro-politics of gendering in networking. *Gender, Work & Organization,* 16(2), 217–237.

Bierema, L. L. (2005). Women's networks: A career development intervention or impediment? *Human Resource Development International,* 8(2), 207–224.

Biggins, J. V. (1999). Making board diversity work. *Corporate Board,* 20(117), 11–16.

Bilimoria, D. (2000). Building the business case for women corporate directors: Women on corporate boards of directors. In R. J. Burke & M. C. Mattis (Eds.) *Women on corporate boards of directors: International challenges and opportunities.* London: Springer, 25–40.

Brammer, S., Millington, A., & Pavelin, S. (2009). Corporate reputation and women on the board. *British Journal of Management,* 20(1), 17–29.

Brass, D. J., Galaskiewicz, J., Greve, H. R., & Tsai, W. (2004). Taking stock of networks and organizations: A multilevel perspective. *Academy of Management Journal,* 47(6), 795–817.

Brickley, J. A., Linck, J. S., & Coles, J. L. (1999). What happens to CEOs after they retire? New evidence on career concerns, horizon problems, and CEO incentives. *Journal of Financial Economics,* 52(3), 341–377.

Brown, S. E. (2016). PhD Barbie gets a makeover! Aesthetic labour in academia. In A. S. Elias, R. Gill, & C. Scharff (Eds.) *Aesthetic labour: Rethinking beauty politics in neoliberalism.* Basingstoke: Palgrave Macmillan.

Brown, S. E., & Kelan, E. K. (2016). There's never been a better time to be a woman? The discursive effects of women on boards research reports. In C. Elliot, V. Stead, S. Mavin, & J. Williams (Eds.) *Gender, media, and organization: Challenging mis(s) representations of women leaders and management.* Charlotte, NC: Information Age Publishing, 77–95.

Brown, S. E., Kelan, E. K., & Humbert, L. A. (2015). *Opening the black box: Comparing women's and men's routes to the boardroom.* Retrieved from https://www.dropbox.com/s/syhsdx64hqtcw4w/Opening%20The%20Black%20Box.pdf?dl=0.

Burgess, Z. M., & Tharenou, P. (2000). What distinguishes women non-executive directors from executive directors? Individual, interpersonal, and organizational factors related to women's appointments to boards. In R. J. Burke & M. C. Mattis (Eds.) *Women on corporate boards of directors: International challenges and opportunities.* London: Springer, 111–127.

Burgess, Z. M., & Tharenou, P. (2002). Women board directors: Characteristics of the few. *Journal of Business Ethics,* 37(1), 39–49.

Burke, R. J. (1997a). Women on corporate boards of directors: A needed resource. *Journal of Business Ethics,* 16(9), 909–915.

Burke, R. J. (1997b). Women directors: Selection, acceptance and benefits of board membership. *Corporate Governance: An International Review,* 5(3), 118–125.

Burke, R. J. (2000). Women on corporate boards of directors: Understanding the context. In R. J. Burke & M. C. Mattis (Eds.) *Women on corporate boards of directors: International challenges and opportunities*. London: Springer, 179–196.

Bushell, M. (2015). *The role of social capital and networking in corporate board selection processes*. Unpublished PhD Thesis, Warwick Business School.

Butler, J. (1990). *Gender trouble: Feminism and the subversion of identity*. London: Routledge.

Calás, M. B., Smircich, L., & Holvino, E. (2014). Theorizing gender-and-organization: Changing times, changing theories. *The Oxford handbook of gender in organizations*. Oxford: Oxford University Press, 17–52.

Carter, D. A., D'Souza, F., Simkins, B. J., & Simpson, W. G. (2010). The gender and ethnic diversity of US boards and board committees and firm financial performance. *Corporate Governance: An International Review*, 18(5), 396–414.

Castilla, E. J., & Benard, S. (2010). The paradox of meritocracy in organizations. *Administrative Science Quarterly*, 55(4), 543–576.

Catalyst (2004). *The bottom line: Connecting corporate performance and gender diversity*. Retrieved from: www.catalyst.org/system/files/The_Bottom_Line_Connecting_Corporate_Performance_and_Gender_Diversity.pdf. May 1, 2019.

Clarke, A. (2019). *Treading the {corporate} board: A critical analysis of organisational diversity discourse*. Unpublished PhD Thesis, University of Essex.

Cockburn, C. (1991). *In the way of women: Men's resistance to sex equality in organizations*. Ithaca, NY: Cornell University Press.

Coverdill, J. E., & Finlay, W. (1998). Fit and skill in employee selection: Insights from a study of headhunters. *Qualitative Sociology*, 21(2), 105–127.

Cross, C., & Armstrong, C. (2008). Understanding the role of networks in collective learning processes: The experiences of women. *Advances in Developing Human Resources*, 10(4), 600–613.

Davies, M. (2011). *Women on boards: February 2011*. Retrieved from: www.gov.uk/government/uploads/system/uploads/attachment_data/file/31480/11-745-women-on-boards.pdf. March 12, 2019.

Davies, M. (2015). *Improving the gender balance on British boards: Women on boards Davies review, five year summary*. Retrieved from: www.gov.uk/government/publications/women-on-boards-5-year-summary-davies-review. May 12, 2019.

de Anca, C., & Gabaldon, P. (2014). Female directors and the media: Stereotypes of board members. *Gender in Management: An International Journal*, 29(6), 334–351.

Devnew, L. E., Le Ber, M. J., Torchia, M., & Burke, R. J. (2018). *More women on boards: An international perspective*. Charlotte, NC: Information Age Publishing.

Doldor, E., Sealy, R., & Vinnicombe, S. (2016). Accidental activists: Headhunters as marginal diversity actors in institutional change towards more women on boards. *Human Resource Management Journal*, 26(3), 285–303.

Doldor, E., Vinnicombe, S., Gaughan, M., & Sealy, R. (2012). Gender diversity on boards: The appointment process and the role of executive search firms, *Equality and Human Rights Commission Research Report Series*, 85.

Dreher, G. F., Lee. J.-Y., & Clerkin, T. A. (2011). Mobility and cash compensation: The moderating effects of gender, race, and executive search firms. *Journal of Management*, 37(3), 651–681.

Eagly, A. H., & Carli, L. L. (2003). The female leadership advantage: An evaluation of the evidence. *The Leadership Quarterly*, 14(6), 807–834.

Eagly, A. H., & Carli, L. L. (2007). Women and the labyrinth of leadership. *Harvard Business Review*, 85(9), 62.

Eagly, A. H., & Karau, S. J. (2002). Role congruity theory of prejudice toward female leaders. *Psychological Review*, 109(3), 573–598.

Eastman, M. T. (2017). *Women on boards: Progress report 2017*. Retrieved from: www.msci.com/documents/10199/239004/MSCI_Women+on+Boards+Progress+Report+2017.pdf/b7786a08-c818-4054-bf3f-ef15fc89537a. February 28, 2019.

Edley, N. (2001). Analysing masculinity: Interpretative repertoires, ideological dilemmas and subject positions. In M. Wetherell, S. Taylor, & S. J. Yates (Eds.) *Discourse as data: A guide for analysis*. London: Sage, 189–228.

Elliott, J. R. (2000). Class, race, and job matching in contemporary urban labor markets. *Social Science Quarterly*, 81(4), 1036–1052.

Ely, R., & Padavic, I. (2007). A feminist analysis of organizational research on sex differences. *Academy of Management Review*, 32(4), 1121–1143.

Eminet, A., & Guedri, Z. (2010). The role of nominating committees and director reputation in shaping the labor market for directors: An empirical assessment. *Corporate Governance: An International Review*, 18(6), 557–574.

Equality and Human Rights Commission (2016). *Inquiry into fairness, transparency and diversity in FTSE 350 board appointments*. Retrieved from: www.equalityhumanrights.com/en/publication-download/inquiry-fairness-transparency-and-diversity-ftse-350-board-appointments. May 1, 2019.

European Commission (2014). *Women and men in leadership positions in the European Union, 2013*. 8 April 2013. Retrieved from: https://op.europa.eu/en/publication-detail/-/publication/d585cda9-7e08-43e8-8bda-487dba4651b5. 8 November, 2019.

European Parliament (2019). *Gender balance on boards*. Retrieved from: www.europarl.europa.eu/legislative-train/theme-area-of-justice-and-fundamental-rights/file-gender-balance-on-boards. February 28, 2019.

Fagan, C., Menèndez, M. G., & Ansón, S. G. (Eds.) (2012). *Women on corporate boards and in top management: European trends and policy*. Basingstoke: Palgrave Macmillan.

Fahlenbrach, R., Low, A., & Stulz, R. M. (2010). Why do firms appoint CEOs as outside directors? *Journal of Financial Economics*, 97(1), 12–32.

Fahlenbrach, R., Minton, B. A. and Pan, C. H. (2011). Former CEO directors: Lingering CEOs or valuable resources? *Review of Financial Studies*, 24(10), 3486–3518.

Fama, E. F. (1980). Agency problems and the theory of the firm. *Journal of Political Economy*, 88(2), 288–307.

Faulconbridge, J., Beaverstock, J., Hall, S., & Hewitson, A. (2009). The 'War for Talent': The gatekeeper role of executive search firms in elite labour markets. *Geoforum*, 40(5), 800–808.

Fich, E. M., & White, L. J. (2005). Why do CEOs reciprocally sit on each other's boards? *Journal of Corporate Finance*, 11(1), 175–195.

Financial Reporting Council (2018). *The UK corporate governance code*. London: Financial Reporting Council.

134 References

Finkelstein, S., Hambrick, D. C., & Cannella, A. A. (2009). *Strategic leadership: Theory and research on executives, top management teams, and boards.* Oxford: Oxford University Press.

Finlay, W., & Coverdill, J. E. (2007). *Headhunters: Matchmaking in the labor market.* Ithaca: Cornell University Press.

Fisher, M. S. (2012). *Wall Street women.* Durham (US): Duke University Press.

Forret, M. L., & Dougherty, T. W. (2001). Correlates of networking behavior for managerial and professional employees. *Group & Organization Management,* 26(3), 283–311.

Foster, D. (2015). *Lean out.* London: Penguin Random House.

Fraser, N. (2009). Feminism, capitalism and the cunning of history. *New Left Review,* 56(March/April 2009), 97–117.

Fraser, N. (2013). *Fortunes of feminism: From State-managed capitalism to neoliberal crisis.* London: Verso Books.

Gabaldon, P., Anca, C., Mateos de Cabo, R., & Gimeno, R. (2016). Searching for women on boards: An analysis from the supply and demand perspective. *Corporate Governance Review,* 24(3), 371–385.

Gaughan, M. (2013). A conceptual framework for reputational capital development: An exploratory study of first-time FTSE 100 NED appointees. Retrieved from: https://dspace.lib.cranfield.ac.uk/handle/1826/8450. November 7, 2019

Gill, R. (1993). Justifying injustice: Broadcasters' accounts of inequality in radio. In E. Burman & I. Parker (Eds.) *Discourse analytic research: Repertoires and readings of texts in action.* London: Routledge, 75–93.

Gill, R. (2000). Discourse analysis. In M. Bauer & G. Gaskell (Eds.) *Qualitative researching with text, image and sound: A practical handbook for social research.* London: Sage, 172–190.

Gill, R. (2002). Cool, creative and egalitarian? Exploring gender in project-based new media work in Europe. *Information, Communication & Society,* 5(1), 70–89.

Gill, R. (2007). *Gender and the media.* Cambridge: Polity Press.

Gill, R., & Orgad, S. (2016). The confidence cult(ure). *Australian Feminist Studies,* 30(86), 324–344.

Granovetter, M. S. (1973). The strength of weak ties. *The American Journal of Sociology,* 78(6), 1360–1380.

Granovetter, M. S. (1983). The strength of weak ties: A network theory revisited. *Sociological Theory,* 1(1983), 201–233.

Gutek, B. A. (1994). *Women in management: Change, progress or an ephemeral phenomenon? The ties that bind:* Proceedings of the global research conference on women and management, School of Business, Carleton University, Ottawa.

Hampton, P., & Alexander, H. (2018). *Hampton Alexander review.* Retrieved from: https://ftsewomenleaders.com/. February 28, 2019.

Hawarden, R. J. (2010). *Women on boards of directors: The origin and structure of gendered small-world and scale-free director glass networks.* Unpublished PhD Thesis, Massey University.

Hawarden, R. J., & Marsland, S. (2011). Locating women board members in gendered director networks. *Gender in Management: An International Journal,* 26(8), 532–549.

Hermalin, B. E., & Weisbach, M. S. (1988). The determinants of board composition. *The RAND Journal of Economics*, 19(4), 589–606.

Hewitt, J. P., & Stokes, R. (1975). Disclaimers. *American Sociological Review*, 40(1), 1–11.

Hewlett, S. A. (2014). *Executive presence: The missing link between merit and success*. London: Harper Business.

Hill, S. (1995). The social organization of boards of directors. *The British Journal of Sociology*, 46(2), 245–278.

Hillman, A. J., Cannella, A. A., & Harris, I. C. (2002). Women and racial minorities in the boardroom: How do directors differ? *Journal of Management*, 28(6), 747–763.

Hillman, A. J., Cannella, A. A., & Paetzold, R. (2000). The resource dependence role of corporate directors: Adaptation of board composition in response to environmental change. *Journal of Management Studies*, 37(2), 235–255.

Hillman, A. J., & Dalziel, T. (2003). Boards of directors and firm performance: Integrating agency and resource dependence perspectives. *Academy of Management Review*, 28(3), 383–396.

Hillman, A. J., Shropshire, C., & Cannella, A. A. (2007). Organizational predictors of women on corporate boards. *Academy of Management Journal*, 50(4), 941–952.

Hillman, A. J., Shropshire, C., Certo, S. T., Dalton, R. D., & Dalton, C. M. (2011). What I like about you: A multilevel study of shareholder discontent with director monitoring. *Organization Science*, 22(3), 675–687.

Holgersson, C. (2013). Recruiting managing directors: Doing homosociality. *Gender, Work & Organization*, 20(4), 454–466.

Hoskisson, R. E., Castleton, M. W., & Withers, M. (2009). Complementarity in monitoring and bonding: More intense monitoring leads to higher executive compensation. *Academy of Management Perspectives*, 23(2), 57–74.

House, J. D., & McGrath, K. (2004). Innovative governance and development in the new Ireland: Social partnership and the integrated approach. *Governance*, 17(1), 29–57.

Humbert, A. L., Kelan, E. K., & Clayton-Hathway, K. (2019). A rights-based approach to board quotas and how hard sanctions work for gender equality. *European Journal of Women's Studies*, 26(4), 447–468

Huse, M. (2008). *The value creating board: Corporate governance and organizational behaviour*. London: Routledge.

Ibarra, H. (1992). Homophily and differential returns: Sex differences in network structure and access in an advertising firm. *Administrative Science Quarterly*, 37(3), 422–447.

Ibarra, H. (1993). Personal networks of women and minorities in management: A conceptual framework. *Academy of Management Review*, 18(1), 56–87.

Ibarra, H. (1995). Race, opportunity, and diversity of social circles in managerial networks. *Academy of Management Journal*, 38(3), 673–703.

Ibarra, H. (1997). Paving an alternative route: Gender differences in managerial networks. *Social Psychology Quarterly*, 60(1), 91–102.

Ibarra, H. (2001). Social networks and gender. In N. J. Smelser & Paul B. Baltes (Eds.) *International encyclopedia of the social & behavioral sciences*. Oxford: Pergamon, 14384–14388.

Ibarra, H., Carter, N. M., & Silva, C. (2010). Why men still get more promotions than women. *Harvard Business Review*, 88(9), 80–85.

Ibarra, H., & Hunter, M. L. (2007). How leaders create and use networks. *Harvard Business Review*, January 2009.

Ibarra, H., Kilduff, M., & Tsai, W. (2005). Zooming in and out: Connecting individuals and collectivities at the frontiers of organizational network research. *Organization Science*, 16(4), 359–371.

Johannisson, B., & Huse, M. (2000). Recruiting outside board members in the small family business: an ideological challenge. *Entrepreneurship & Regional Development*, 12(4), 353–378.

Johnson, J. L., Daily, C. M., & Ellstrand, A. E. (1996). Boards of directors: A review and research agenda. *Journal of Management*, 22(3), 409–438.

Johnson, S. K., Hekman, D. R., & Chan, E. T. (2016). If there's only one woman in your candidate pool, there's statistically no chance she'll be hired. *Harvard Business Review*, April 2016

Kaczmarek, S., Kimino, S., & Pye, A. (2012). Antecedents of board composition: The role of nomination committees. *Corporate Governance: An International Review*, 20(5), 474–489.

Kanter, R. M. (1977). *Men and women of the corporation*. London: Basic Books.

Kelan, E. K. (2009a). Gender fatigue: The ideological dilemma of gender neutrality and discrimination in organizations. *Canadian Journal of Administrative Sciences*, 26(3), 197–210.

Kelan, E. K. (2009b). *Performing gender at work*. Basingstoke: Palgrave Macmillan.

Kelan, E. K. (2010), Gender logic and (un)doing gender at work. *Gender, Work and Organization*, 17(2), 174–194.

Kelan, E. K. (2013). The becoming of business bodies: Gender, appearance, and leadership development. *Management Learning*, 44(1), 45–61.

Kelan, E. K. (2014). From biological clocks to unspeakable inequalities: The intersectional positioning of young professionals. *British Journal of Management*, 25(4), 790–804.

Kelan, E. K., & Jones, R. D. (2010). Gender and the MBA. *Academy of Management Learning & Education*, 9(1), 26–43.

Khurana, R. (2002). *Searching for a corporate savior: The irrational quest for charismatic CEOs*. Princeton: Princeton University Press.

Kirsch, A. (2018). The gender composition of corporate boards: A review and research agenda. *The Leadership Quarterly*, 29(2), 346–364.

Kirsch, A., & Sauerborn, E. (2019). *Revolution from above? Women directors and gender equality in organizations*. Unpublished working paper.

Kor, Y. Y., & Misangyi, V. F. (2008). Outside directors' industry-specific experience and firms' liability of newness. *Strategic Management Journal*, 29(12), 1345–1355.

Korn/Ferry Institute (2012). *What makes an exceptional independent non executive director?* Retrieved from: https://www.kornferry.com/institute/459-what-makes-an-exceptional-independent-non-executive-director. November 9, 2019.

Lowe, S., Brown, S., & Kobel, Y. (2016). *The future of governance: One small step . . . corporate governance review*. Grant Thornton Governance Institute. Retrieved from: https://www.grantthornton.co.uk/globalassets/1.-member-firms/united-kingdom/pdf/publication/2016/2016-corporate-governance-review.pdf. November 9, 2019.

Lowe, S., Brown, S., & Kobel, Y. (2017). *Grant Thornton corporate governance review 2017*. Grant Thornton Governance Institute. Retrieved from: https://www.grantthornton.co.uk/globalassets/1.-member-firms/united-kingdom/pdf/publication/corporate-governance-review-2017.pdf. November 9, 2019.

Lowe, S., Brown, S., & Kobel, Y. (2018). *Grant Thornton corporate governance review 2018*. Grant Thornton Governance Institute. Retrieved from: https://www.grantthornton.co.uk/globalassets/1.-member-firms/united-kingdom/pdf/documents/corporate-governance-review-2018.pdf. November 7, 2019.

Lowe, S., Fargeot, C. & Kobel, Y. (2015). *Grant Thornton corporate governance review 2015*. Grant Thornton Governance Institute. Retrieved from: https://www.grantthornton.co.uk/globalassets/1.-member-firms/united-kingdom/pdf/publication/2015/uk-corporate-governance-review-and-trends-2015.pdf. November 9, 2019.

Martin, P. Y. (2001). Mobilizing masculinities': Women's experiences of men at work. *Organization*, 8(4), 587–618.

Martin, P. Y. (2003). "Said and Done" versus "Saying and Doing" gendering practices, practicing gender at work. *Gender & Society*, 17(3), 342–366.

Matsa, D., & Miller, A. (2013). A female style in corporate leadership? Evidence from quotas. *American Economic Journal: Applied Economics*, 5(3), 136–169.

Mattis, M. C. (1993). Women directors: Progress and opportunities for the future. *Business and the Contemporary World*, 5(3), 140–156.

Mattis, M. C. (2000). Women corporate directors in the United States. In R. J. Burke and M. C. Mattis (Eds.) *Women on corporate boards of directors*. London: Springer, 43–56.

Mavin, S. (2006). Venus envy 2: Sisterhood, queen bees and female misogyny in management. *Women in Management Review*, 21(5), 349–364.

Mavin, S. (2008). Queen bees, wannabees and afraid to bees: No more 'best enemies' for women in management? *British Journal of Management*, 19(s1), S75–S84.

Mavin, S., & Grandy, G. (2012). Doing gender well and differently in management. *Gender in Management: An International Journal*, 27(4), 218–231.

Mavin, S., & Grandy, G. (2013). Doing gender well and differently in dirty work: The case of exotic dancing. *Gender, Work & Organization*, 20(3), 232–251.

Mavin, S., & Grandy, G. (2016a). A theory of Abject Appearance: Women elite leaders' intra-gender 'management' of bodies and appearance. *Human Relations*, 69(5), 1095–1120.

Mavin, S., & Grandy, G. (2016b). Women elite leaders doing respectable business femininity: How privilege is conferred, contested and defended through the body. *Gender, Work & Organization*, 23(4), 379–396.

Mavin, S., Grandy, G., & Williams, J. (2014). Experiences of women elite leaders doing gender: Intra-gender micro-violence between women. *British Journal of Management*, 25(3), 439–455.

McCauley, C. D. (2004). Successful and unsuccessful leadership. In J. Antonakis, A. T. Cianciolo, & R. J. Sternberg (Eds.) *The nature of leadership*. Thousand Oaks: Sage, 199–221.

McDonald, S. (2010). Right place, right time: Serendipity and informal job matching. *Socio-Economic Review*, 8(2), 307–331.

McDonald, S., & Elder, G. H. (2006). When does social capital matter? Non-searching for jobs across the life course. *Social Forces*, 85(1), 521–549.

McDowell, L. (1997). *Capital culture: Gender at work in the city*. Oxford: Blackwell.

McDowell, L. (1998). Elites in the city of London: Some methodological considerations. *Environment and Planning A*, 30(12), 2133–2146.

McGregor, J. (2000). Stereotypes and symbolic annihilation: Press constructions of women at the top. *Women in Management Review*, 15(5/6), 290–295.

McGuire, G. M. (2000). Gender, race, ethnicity, and networks the factors affecting the status of employees' network members. *Work and Occupations*, 27(4), 501–524.

McKinsey & Company (2007). Gender diversity, a corporate performance driver. *Women Matter*, 1. Retrieved from: www.mckinsey.com/features/women_matter. May 1, 2019.

McKinsey & Company (2008). Female leadership, a competitive edge for the future. *Women Matter*, 2. Retrieved from: www.mckinsey.com/features/women_matter. May 1, 2019.

McKinsey & Company (2010). Women at the top of corporations: Making it happen. *Women Matter*, 4. Retrieved from: www.mckinsey.com/features/women_matter. May 1, 2019.

McRobbie, A. (2009). *The aftermath of feminism: Gender, culture and social change*. London: Sage.

McRobbie, A. (2013). Feminism, the family and the new 'mediated' maternalism. *New Formations*, 80(1), 119–137.

Menèndez, M. C. G., & González, L. M. (2012). Spain on the Norwegian pathway: Towards a gender-balanced presence of women on corporate boards. In C. Fagan, M. González Menèndez, S. Gómez Ansón (Eds.) *Women on corporate boards and in top management – European Trends and Policy*. London: Palgrave Macmillan, 169–197.

Meriläinen, S., Tienari, J., & Valtonen, A. (2013). Headhunters and the 'ideal' executive body. *Organization*, 22(1), 3–22.

Monks, R. A. G., & Minow, N. (2004). *Corporate governance* (Vol. 3). Malden, MA: Blackwell.

Nicholson, G. J., & Kiel, G. C. (2004). A framework for diagnosing board effectiveness. *Corporate Governance: An International Review*, 12(4), 442–460.

Nielsen, S., & Huse, M. (2010). The contribution of women on boards of directors: Going beyond the surface. *Corporate Governance: An International Review*, 18(2), 136–148.

Noon, M. (2007). The fatal flaws of diversity and the business case for ethnic minorities. *Work, Employment and Society*, 21(4), 773–784.

O'Neil, D., Hopkins, M., & Sullivan, S. (2011). Do women's networks help advance women's careers? Differences in perceptions of female workers and top leadership. *Career Development International*, 16(7), 733–754.

Ornstein, N. J., & Schenkenberg, A. L. (1995). The 1995 congress: The first hundred days and beyond. *Political Science Quarterly*, 110(2), 183–206.

Peterson, C. A., & Philpot, J. (2007). Women's roles on US Fortune 500 boards: Director expertise and committee memberships. *Journal of Business Ethics*, 72(2), 177–196.

Post, C., & Byron, K. (2014). Women on boards and firm financial performance: A meta-analysis. *Academy of Management Journal*, 58(5), 1546–1571.

Probyn, E. (2005). *Blush: Faces of shame*. Minneapolis: University of Minnesota Press.

Prügl, E. (2012). If Lehman brothers had been Lehman sisters . . .: Gender and myth in the aftermath of the financial crisis. *International Political Sociology*, 6(1), 21–35.

Prügl, E. (2015). Neoliberalising feminism. *New Political Economy*, 20(4), 614–631.

Pye, A. (2000). Changing scenes in, from and outside the boardroom: UK corporate governance in practice from 1989 to 1999. *Corporate Governance: An International Review*, 8(4), 335–346.

Pye, A. (2001). A study in studying corporate boards over time: Looking backwards to move forwards. *British Journal of Management*, 12(1), 33–45.

Pye, A. (2002). The changing power of 'explanations': Directors, academics and their sensemaking from 1989 to 2000. *Journal of Management Studies*, 39(7), 907–925.

Riley, S. C. (2003). The management of the traditional male role: A discourse analysis of the constructions and functions of provision. *Journal of Gender Studies*, 12(2), 99–113.

Roberts, A. (2015). The political economy of "Transnational Business Feminism": Problematizing the corporate-led gender equality agenda. *International Feminist Journal of Politics*, 17(2), 209–231.

Rottenberg, C. (2014). The rise of neoliberal feminism. *Cultural Studies*, 28(3), 418–437.

Rottenberg, C. (2018). *The rise of neoliberal feminism*. Oxford: Oxford University Press.

Ruigrok, W., Peck, S., & Tacheva, S. (2007). Nationality and gender diversity on Swiss corporate boards. *Corporate Governance: An International Review*, 15(4), 546–557.

Ruigrok, W., Peck, S., Tacheva, S., Greve, P., & Hu, Y. (2006). The determinants and effects of board nomination committees. *Journal of Management & Governance*, 10(2), 119–148.

Rutherford, S. (2001). Organizational cultures, women managers and exclusion. *Women in Management Review*, 16(8), 371–382.

Sandberg, S. (2013). *Lean in—Women, work and the will to lead*. New York: Random House.

Savage, M. (2015). *Social class in the 21st century*. London: Penguin.

Savage, M., Devine, F., Cunningham, N., Taylor, M., Li, Y., Hjellbrekke, J., & Miles, A. (2013). A new model of social class? Findings from the BBC's Great British Class Survey experiment. *Sociology*, 47(2), 219–250.

Savage, M., & Williams, K. (2008). Elites: Remembered in capitalism and forgotten by social sciences. *The Sociological Review*, 56(s1), 1–24.

Scharff, C. (2012). *Repudiating feminism: Young women in a neoliberal world*. Farnham: Ashgate.

Scott, D. B. (1998). Women at the intersection of business and government: Are they in places of power? *Sociological Spectrum*, 18(3), 333–363.

Sealy, R. (2010). Changing perceptions of meritocracy in senior women's careers. *Gender in Management*, 25(3), 184–197.

Sealy, R., & Doherty, N. (2012). *Women in finance: A springboard to corporate board positions?* The Association of Chartered Certified Accountants (ACCA). Retrieved from: www.accaglobal.com/content/dam/acca/global/PDF-technical/human-capital/pol-tp-cgs.pdf. May 1, 2019.

Sealy, R., Doldor, E., Vinnicombe, S., Terjesen, S., Anderson, D., & Atewologun, D. (2017). Expanding the notion of dialogic trading zones for impactful research: The case of women on boards research. *British Journal of Management*, 28(1), 64–83.

Seierstad, C. (2016). Beyond the business case: The need for both utility and justice rationales for increasing the share of women on boards. *Corporate Governance: An International Review*, 24(4), 390–405.

Seierstad, C., & Opsahl, T. (2011). For the few not the many? The effects of affirmative action on presence, prominence, and social capital of women directors in Norway. *Scandinavian Journal of Management*, 27(1), 44–54.

Seierstad, C., Warner-Søderholm, G., Torchia, M., & Huse, M. (2017). Increasing the number of women on boards: The role of actors and processes. *Journal of Business Ethics*, 141(2), 289–315.

Sheridan, A. (2001). A view from the top: Women on the boards of public companies. *Corporate Governance*, 1(1), 8–15.

Sheridan, A., McKenzie, F., & Still, L. (2011). Complex and contradictory: The doing of gender on regional development boards. *Gender, Work and Organization*, 18(3), 282–297.

Sheridan, A., & Milgate, G. (2005). Accessing board positions: A comparison of female and male board members' views. *Corporate Governance: An International Review*, 13(6), 847–855.

Sheridan, A., Ross-Smith, A., & Lord, L. (2015). Women on boards in Australia: Achieving real change or more of the same? In *Handbook of gendered careers in management: Getting in, getting on, getting out*. Cheltenham: Edward Elgar Publishing, 322 –340.

Shilton, J., McGregor, J., & Tremaine, M. (2010). Feminizing the boardroom. *Gender in Management: An International Journal*, 25(4), 275–284.

Simpson, R., & Kumra, S. (2016). The Teflon effect: When the glass slipper meets merit. *Gender in Management: An International Journal*, 31(8), 562–576.

Simpson, R., Ross-Smith, A., & Lewis, P. (2010). Merit, special contribution and choice: How women negotiate between sameness and difference in their organizational lives. *Gender in Management: An International Journal*, 25(3), 198–207.

Sinclair, A. (2011). Leading with body. In E. Jeanes, D. Knights, & P. Martin (Eds.) *Handbook of gender, work and organization*. London: John Wiley and Sons, 117–130.

Singh, V., Terjesen, S., & Vinnicombe, S. (2008). Newly appointed directors in the boardroom: How do women and men differ? *European Management Journal*, 26(1), 48–58.

Singh, V., & Vinnicombe, S. (2004). Why so few women directors in top UK boardrooms? Evidence and theoretical explanations. *Corporate Governance: An International Review*, 12(4), 479–488.

Stern, I., & Westphal, J. D. (2010). Stealthy footsteps to the boardroom: Executives' backgrounds, sophisticated interpersonal influence behavior, and board appointments. *Administrative Science Quarterly*, 55(2), 278–319.

Stevenson, W. B., & Radin, R. F. (2009). Social capital and social influence on the board of directors. *Journal of Management Studies*, 46(1), 16–44.

Struber, M. (2012). *Gender diversity and corporate performance*, Credit Suisse Research Institute. Retrieved from: www.calstrs.com/sites/main/files/file-attach ments/csri_gender_diversity_and_corporate_performance.pdf. May 1, 2019.

Talmud, I., & Izraeli, D. N. (1999). The relationship between gender and performance issues of concern to directors: Correlates or institution? *Journal of Organizational Behavior*, 20(4), 459–474.

Taylor, S. (2001). Locating and conducting discourse analytic research. In M. Wetherell, S. Taylor, & S. Yates (Eds.) *Discourse as data: A guide for analysis*. London: Sage, 5–48.

Terjesen, S., Sealy, R., & Singh, V. (2009). Women directors on corporate boards: A review and research agenda. *Corporate Governance: An International Review*, 17(3), 320–337.

Terjesen, S., Singh, V., & Vinnicombe, S. (2008). Do women still lack the "right" kinds of human capital for directorships on the FTSE100 corporate board? In S. Vinnicombe, V. Singh, R. Burke, D. Bilimoria, & M. Huse (Eds.) *Women on corporate boards of directors: International research and practice*. Cheltenham: Edward Elgar Publishing.

Tienari, J., Meriläinen, S., Holgersson, C., & Bendl, R. (2013). And then there are none: On the exclusion of women in processes of executive search. *Gender in Management: An International Journal*, 28(1), 43–62.

Torchia, M., Calabrò, A., & Huse, M. (2011). Women directors on corporate boards: From tokenism to critical mass. *Journal of Business Ethics*, 102(2), 299–317.

Tricker, R. I., & Lee, K. (1997). Assessing directors' core competencies—The case of the mass transit railway corporation, Hong Kong. *Corporate Governance: An International Review*, 5(2), 87–101.

van den Brink, M., & Benschop, Y. (2009). Gender in academic networking: The role of gatekeepers in professorial recruitment. *Journal of Management Studies*, 51(3), 460–492.

van den Brink, M., & Benschop, Y. (2012). Slaying the seven-headed Dragon: The quest for gender change in academia. *Gender, Work & Organization*, 19(1), 71–92.

van den Brink, M., & Benschop, Y. (2014). Gender in academic networking: The role of gatekeepers in professorial recruitment. *Journal of Management Studies*, 51(3), 460–492.

Vinicombe, S., Sealy, R., Graham, J., & Doldor, E. (2010). *The female FTSE board report 2010: Opening up the appointment process*. Cranfield International Centre for Women Leaders. Retrieved from: https://dspace.lib.cranfield. ac.uk/handle/1826/4899. May 1, 2019.

Vinkenburg, C. J., Van Engen, M. L., Eagly, A. H., & Johannesen-Schmidt, M. C. (2011). An exploration of stereotypical beliefs about leadership styles: Is transformational leadership a route to women's promotion? *The Leadership Quarterly*, 22(1), 10–21.

Wajcman, J. (1999). *Managing like a man: Women and men in corporate management*. Cambridge: Polity Press.

Walt, N., & Ingley, C. (2003). Board dynamics and the influence of professional background, gender and ethnic diversity of directors. *Corporate Governance: An International Review*, 11(3), 218–234.

Wang, M., & Kelan, E. K. (2013). The gender quota and female leadership—Effects of the Norwegian gender quota on board chairs and CEOs. *Journal of Business Ethics*, 117(3), 449–466.

Warhurst, C., & Nickson, D. (2007). Employee experience of aesthetic labour in retail and hospitality. *Work, Employment & Society*, 21(1), 103–120.

West, C., & Zimmerman, D. H. (1987). Doing gender. *Gender & Society*, 1(2), 125–151.

Westphal, J. D. (1998). Board games: How CEOs adapt to increases in structural board independence from management. *Administrative Science Quarterly*, 43(3), 511–537.

Westphal, J. D. (1999). Collaboration in the boardroom: Behavioral and performance consequences of CEO-board social ties. *Academy of Management Journal*, 42(1), 7–24.

Westphal, J. D. (2010). An impression management perspective on job design: The case of corporate directors. *Journal of Organizational Behavior*, 31(2–3), 319–327.

Westphal, J. D., & Graebner, M. E. (2010). A matter of appearances: How corporate leaders manage the impressions of financial analysts about the conduct of their boards. *Academy of Management Journal*, 53(1), 15–44.

Westphal, J. D., & Khanna, P. (2003). Keeping directors in line: Social distancing as a control mechanism in the corporate elite. *Administrative Science Quarterly*, 48(3), 361–398.

Westphal, J. D., & Milton, L. P. (2000). How experience and network ties affect the influence of demographic minorities on corporate boards. *Administrative Science Quarterly*, 45(2), 366–398.

Westphal, J. D., & Stern, I. (2006). The other pathway to the boardroom: Interpersonal influence behavior as a substitute for elite credentials and majority status in obtaining board appointments. *Administrative Science Quarterly*, 51(2), 169–204.

Westphal, J. D., & Stern, I. (2007). Flattery will get you everywhere (especially if you are a male Caucasian): How ingratiation, boardroom behavior, and demographic minority status affect additional board appointments at US companies. *Academy of Management Journal*, 50(2), 267–288.

Wetherell, M. (1998). Positioning and interpretative repertoires: Conversation analysis and post-structuralism in dialogue. *Discourse & Society*, 9(3), 387–412.

Wirz, M. (2014). *The paradox of embodiment in leadership: Bringing the body into executive search*. Paper presented at bi-annual gender work and organization conference, Keele University, UK.

Witz, A., Warhurst, C., & Nickson, D. (2003). The labour of aesthetics and the aesthetics of organization. *Organization*, 10(1), 33–54.

Withers, M. C., Hillman, A. J., & Cannella, A. A. (2012). A multidisciplinary review of the director selection literature. *Journal of Management*, 38(1), 243–277.

Zajac, E. J., & Westphal, J. D. (1996). Director reputation, CEO-board power, and the dynamics of board interlocks. *Administrative Science Quarterly*, 41(3), 507–529.

Zattoni, A., & Cuomo, F. (2010). How independent, competent and incentivized should non-executive directors be? An empirical investigation of good governance codes. *British Journal of Management*, 21(1), 63–79.

Zhu, D. H., Shen, W., & Hillman, A. J. (2014). Recategorization into the in-group the appointment of demographically different new directors and their subsequent positions on corporate boards. *Administrative Science Quarterly*, 59(2), 240–270.

Zorn, D. M. (2004). Here a chief, there a chief: The rise of the CFO in the American firm. *American Sociological Review*, 69(3), 345–364.

Index

2008 financial crisis 10, 13

A-B-A structure 102, 104
accidental activism 17, 65
Acker, J. 13, 24
Adams, R. B. 7, 8, 15, 16
Adams, S. M. 20
Adamson, M. 39, 82
aesthetic labour 84; *see also*
  appearance, women's
affective connections 71, 90
age of applicants 25–26, 33
aggressiveness 39
Ahern, K. R. 8, 10, 118
Albright, Madeleine viii, 67, 68, 79
Alexander, H. 3, 8
all-men private clubs 19
all-women networks 21–22, 66–77, 79
Alternative Investment Market (AIM)
  46, 80n1
Alvesson, M. 78, 112, 113
analytical thinking 12
appearance, women's 13, 14, 46–47,
  51, 84, 111, 122, 124
appointment processes: challenging
  current 89, 126, 128;
  democratisation of 23n8; future
  directions for research 124;
  justifications for continuation of
  current model 119–120; opacity
  of 3, 15, 17, 18, 53, 56, 105–106,
  113, 119–120; research literature
  15–18; research process 4–5;
  rigorous appointment processes
  16, 17, 18; role of headhunters 65;
  transparency 120; *see also* barriers
  to entry
arrogance 45
assertiveness 39

Atewologun, D. 123
Augar, P. 17, 57, 92, 117, 120
awards, winning 25

background checks 28
barriers to entry: heroic narratives about
  overcoming 82, 91, 105; internal
  barriers 81, 87, 91, 105, 116; men's
  informal networks exclude women
  19, 78; networking 19, 78, 81, 87,
  89, 115; to senior roles generally 15;
  structural 89, 116–117
Beaverstock, J. V. 17, 65, 78, 92,
  112, 113
Benard, S. 112
Bennett, T. 119
Benschop, Y. 18, 19, 20–21, 22, 71,
  112, 113–114, 124
Bierema, L. L. 21, 22, 77, 79, 115
BoardEx 55
boards of directors, definitions of 6–7
Brexit 2, 128
Brickley, J. A. 109
Brown, S. E. 18, 30, 54, 74–75, 80n1,
  117, 124
Burgess, Z. M. 8, 9, 19, 20
Bushell, M. 9, 11, 16, 18, 19
business case for women on boards 7,
  8–9, 13, 50, 118, 127
business judgement skills 40
Butler, J. 9

Calás, M. B. 9, 126
campaign networking 83
career achievements, previous 25; *see
  also* 'right' experience discourse
career narratives 25, 27
care work/childcare responsibilities
  2, 25–26

Carli, L. L. 13, 40
Castilla, E. J. 112
CEO (Chief Executive Officer) 3, 7,
11, 14, 16, 31, 33, 42–43, 90–91;
see also C-suite roles
CFO (Chief Financial Officer) 3, 7,
31–32, 33, 48; *see also* C-suite roles
chair of the board: as gatekeeper
of the board 60; influence on
perceptions of ideal board members
32; interviewing prospective
members 43, 44; networks 18; and
nomination committees 16; role of
xi; subjective decision-making 110;
visibility to 72–73
challenging the board 38–40, 42, 45,
49–50, 110
characteristics of board members
9, 12–13; *see also* ideal board
members
childcare responsibilities/care work 2,
25–26
choosiness 95–98, 106–107, 116, 120
Clarke, A. 9, 128
closure mechanisms 52
clothing 46–47, 51, 122; *see also*
appearance, women's
clubs 19; *see also* Old Boys' networks
cold-calling approaches 54, 57, 59,
63, 78
collaborative leadership 13
collective nature of a board 43, 50
combativeness 39, 40, 50
commodification of relationship 55, 77
communication skills 12
competence as a director 14, 15, 17
competition for roles 58, 117
confidence cult(ure) 116
consensus-based decision making 14
conservatism 46, 47, 48, 51, 122, 124
conversation analysis methods
123–124
corporate elites 119, 124–125
corporate feminism 67–68, 82, 88,
106, 117
Corporate Governance Code 16, 28
correlation versus causation 8
co-sponsorship 114
courage 38–40
critical feminist theory 19, 126, 127
C-suite roles 27, 31–32, 43; *see also*
CEO (Chief Executive Officer);
CFO (Chief Financial Officer)

cultural meanings 78
cultural norms 120
culture of being 125
Cuomo, F. 11
curiosity 38, 39, 41
cyclical truth effects 29, 51, 67, 109

Dalziel, T. 9, 11, 12
Davies' Review 2, 3, 8, 17, 29, 65,
80n1, 101, 107–108, 118, 125, 127
desperate woman stereotypes 59, 61,
114, 122
disclaimers (discourse strategy) 59,
102, 103, 104, 118
discourse analysis 4, 123
dis-identification 49
Dittmar, A. K. 8, 10, 118
diversity: all-women networking
events 72; and the business case
for women on boards 127; and
experience/skills 29; men's views
on 101–102, 107–108; networking
66–67; and nomination committees
16; restricted by narrow 'ideal
candidate' definitions 4; and
tokenistic views of women on
boards 118
Doherty, N. 10, 11, 14, 27, 48, 49
'doing time' versus learning skills 32
Doldor, E. 3, 10, 14, 15, 16, 17, 18,
50, 51, 53, 65, 123, 127, 128
domestic responsibilities 2, 26
double bind 13, 116, 121
Dreher, G. F. 17, 18
dress/clothing 46–47, 51, 122; *see
also* appearance, women's
due diligence 96, 97
Dunkley Jones, R. 68

Eagly, A. H. 13, 40
'easier for women' discourse 98–104,
107–108, 117–118, 123, 126
Eastman, M. T. 7, 8
effective boards, expanding research
to include 123–124
elite identities: and ability to be choosy
116; corporate elites 119, 124–125;
and gender 122; and the ideal board
member 29–30, 48–49, 52, 110,
112; lean-in discourse 116–117;
networking 55, 63, 73, 78, 80;
sitting back discourse 92, 95,

106–107; wealth elites 119; women in elite roles generally 120–121
embodied femininity 122
embodied fit 124
embodied leadership 122
emotional connections 71, 90
emotional intelligence 50
'emotional' nature of women 11
Equality and Human Rights Commission (EHRC) 14, 15, 53
essentialist notions of gender 9
ethnographic research 121
European Parliament 8
executive board members 3, 7; *see also* CEO (Chief Executive Officer); CFO (Chief Financial Officer); C-suite roles
executive committees, gender balance of 3
'executive presence' 13
executive search firms *see* headhunters; search/recruitment firms
experience requirements: previous board experience 10, 30–33, 109; the 'right fit' 43; women's compared to men's 9, 11, 15, 74; 'wrong' experience discourse 33–35, 36–37, 103, 110; *see also* 'right' experience discourse

face, maintaining 107
Fahlenbrach, R. 10, 111
failure 88–91, 95–96, 102, 105, 107, 116–117, 120
Faulconbridge, J. 17, 21, 22, 23n7, 23n8, 29, 35, 37, 51, 52, 62
favour rendering 12, 64, 84, 85
female friendships 19–20, 21; *see also* women-women relationships
femininity: downplaying 48; embodied 122; feminine leadership styles 40, 50; and the Handbag Society 72; negative connotations 122; and networking 19–20, 87; respectable business femininity 11, 51, 121–122; and socio-economic background 124; usually associated with passivity 106; women need to perform 13, 111, 114
feminism: corporate 67–68, 82, 88, 106, 117; critical feminist theory 19, 126, 127; gender equality aims 66, 82, 124; men talking about 102;

neoliberal 21, 39, 51, 82–84, 105, 115, 121–122; pseudo- 79; radical feminist theory 126
Fich, E. M. 10, 109
finance industries 10–11, 112, 121
financial crisis (2008) 10, 13
Financial Reporting Council (FRC) 7, 16, 38, 65
financial skills/qualifications/experience 10–11, 27–28, 29, 103
Financial Times NED diploma 74–75
Fisher, M. S. 112, 113, 121
fitting in discourses 46–48, 51, 52, 109–112
fit with the current board 13–15, 24, 41–46, 50, 52, 97, 123
Flynn, P. M. 20
Foster, D. 91, 105, 116, 117
Foucault, M. 9
friendships 19–20, 21, 55–56, 57, 62, 77
FTSE 100 (Financial Times Stock Exchange 100) 2, 3, 8, 9, 10, 14, 18, 27–28, 60, 65, 80n1
FTSE 350 (Financial Times Stock Exchange 350) 4, 16, 23n7, 33, 80n1, 100, 117, 119
functionalism 9
future directions for research 123–125

game, playing the: ideal board members 32, 51; lean-in discourse 81, 85, 86–88, 89, 105, 106, 115; networking 65, 68, 70; privilege 119; sitting back discourse 94
gatekeeper roles: appointment rests on visibility to 18, 20, 53, 112–113, 114; gendered networking 22, 115; headhunters as 63, 75; networking 22, 60, 74; and sponsors 79; and women's networks 70
Gaughan, M. 10, 14, 15, 18, 19, 28, 36, 51, 53
gender: and corporate elites 119; definitions 9; doing/performing 9, 13, 48, 50, 71, 111; essentialist notions 9; and leadership 2, 12–13, 39, 50; and the need for providing challenge to the board 39; and networks 4, 114, 115; and privilege 121; and social networks 19–20; transmission of gender knowledge 68; 'wild cards' 36

gender equality 66, 82, 124
gender pay gap 128
gentlemanly capitalism 17, 92, 117, 120
gentlemanly interaction modes 57
Germany 7
Gill, R. 2, 59, 82, 91, 102, 104, 109, 116, 117, 118
glass ceiling 88, 121, 124
golden skirts phenomenon 10
Grandy, G. 13, 40, 50, 51, 55, 72, 77, 111, 120, 121, 122, 124
Granovetter, M. S. 19, 23n10, 113

Hampton, P. 3, 8
Hampton Alexander Review (2018) 3, 8
Handbag Society 70–77, 87, 122
hard work narratives 82–83, 84, 85, 90–91, 95, 121–122
'having it all' discourse 26
Hawarden, R. J. 10
headhunters: advice on appearance 46–47; denigrating the role of 88; female 101; as gatekeepers 63, 75; influence on perceptions of ideal board members 32, 51–52, 75; men's 'sitting back' 92; and neoliberal feminism 84; networking 17, 54, 57, 63–65, 66–67, 68; New Girls' Networks 66–67, 68; and personal recommendations 21, 62–65, 78; preference for previous board experience 30; statistics on usage 23n7; subjectivity in appointment processes 14, 17–18, 28, 30, 34; translating experience into 'right' experience 34, 110; and transparency in appointment processes 16, 17; waiting to be approached by 59, 62–63, 78, 92, 113, 116; 'wild cards' 35–37; working (within) the system 86–88
heroic narratives 82–86, 91, 103
Hewitt, J. P. 102, 118
Hill, S. 10, 14, 110
Hillman, A. J. 9, 10, 11, 12, 23n5
Holgersson, C. 19, 92, 110
HR (Human Resources) backgrounds 35, 110
human capital 6, 9–12, 15, 25, 67, 109–112, 123
Humbert, L. A. 2, 118, 126
hundred-day targets 55
Hunter, M. L. 19
hygiene factors 46

Ibarra, H. 19, 20, 21, 64, 71, 78, 113, 114
ideal board members 24–52, 101, 109–112
ideal workers 24
impression management 27, 29, 52, 61, 111, 113, 123
independent directors 12, 16, 22n1
individualised discourses 9, 41, 83–89, 105–106, 110, 115, 119–120
influence, ability to 12, 38
informality of boards 43, 50
informal networking 19, 50–51, 53, 57–62, 92–93, 106, 115–116
information overload 23n8
inquisitiveness 38–40, 41
inspirational/visionary qualities 12
instinct 97
instrumentalism 20, 70
intellectual abilities 42, 43, 49
internal barriers 81, 87, 91, 105, 116
interpersonal skills 12, 38, 40–41, 42, 43, 50
interviews for roles 43, 44, 46
introductions, personal 62–65, 78
intrusiveness 59; *see also* pushiness

job descriptions 52

Kelan, E. K. 2, 8, 13, 39, 68, 79, 82, 106, 108, 111, 118
Kirsch, A. 2, 6, 7, 9, 22, 128
Kumra, S. 111

Lagarde, Christine 67, 68
language of the board, speaking 11
leadership and women, generally 2, 12–13, 13, 39, 50
Lean In (Sandberg) 2, 82
lean-in discourse 2, 81–91, 105–106, 115–118, 122–123
legal backgrounds 34–35, 50, 75, 103, 110
leverage points 55
'liability of newness' 10
life history methodologies 27
linear narratives of progress 91
LinkedIn 23n8, 55
longitudinal research method x, 1, 4–5, 81, 114
Lowe, S. 7, 10, 16, 48, 65, 112
luck 54, 64, 84, 91–92, 93

make-up 47, 83–84; *see also*
    appearance, women's; clothing
marital status 26
Marsland, S. 10
Martin, P. Y. 9, 19
masculinity: and the 'ideal' board
    member 110; leadership 40;
    masculine leadership traits 40;
    masculinisation of power 13;
    networking practices 103; in senior
    positions generally 13; women need
    to perform 13, 40, 110, 111
maternity leave 26
Mattis, M. C. 11, 18
Mavin, S. 13, 19, 21, 40, 50, 51,
    55, 68, 71, 72, 77, 111, 120,
    121, 122, 124
MBAs 9
McDowell, L. 13, 27, 120, 121
McGregor, J. 14, 20
McRobbie, A. 82, 111
men: networking 74–75; perception
    that it is easier for women to
    get roles 4, 98–104, 124–128;
    recommending each other 69; as
    recruiters 17; as reference 'norm'
    12, 13, 17; sitting back discourse
    82, 91–104; still the majority of
    new appointments to boards 3;
    unconscious homophily 69
mentors 21; *see also* sponsorship
Meriläinen, S. 14, 17, 111
meritocracy: and the business case
    for women on boards 127; and the
    effective board 123; and elitism 119;
    'fitting in with the current board'
    narrative 14, 110; ideal board
    members 39, 43, 52, 111–112, 120,
    125; and male privilege 121; and
    networks 19, 64–65; presupposition
    of 11; sitting back discourse 91,
    102, 106, 108; using a search firm
    16; women emphasise 123; women-
    on-boards agenda 118
meta-shame 90
#MeToo 128
Milgate, G. 9, 12, 18, 49
Morgan Stanley Capital International
    All-Country World index (MSCI
    ACWI) 23n2
multiple board memberships, holding 7

narrow briefs 4, 17, 33, 42, 52, 64,
    109, 123

natural posture 38
neoliberal feminism 21, 39, 51,
    82–84, 105, 115, 121–122
networking practices approach
    20, 114
networks: active versus passive
    networking 81, 92, 94, 106–107;
    all-women networks 21–22, 66–77,
    79; art of networking 53–80;
    campaign networking 83; deliberate
    versus happenstance 93; and
    gender 4, 114, 115; headhunters
    17, 54, 57, 63–65, 66–67, 68;
    informal networking 19, 50–51,
    53, 57–62, 92–93, 106, 115–116;
    need for mixed male-female 76;
    networking as 'waste of time' 70,
    72–73, 76, 78, 84, 115; networking
    as work 55, 60, 83–84, 92, 113,
    116; networking events 70–77;
    networking websites 55; New
    Girls' Networks 66–69; Old Boys'
    networks 17, 19, 53, 69, 75–76,
    79, 92, 115, 120; one-on-one
    networking 74–75, 115; research
    literature 18–22; social network
    theories 19, 21; subtle networking
    53, 57–62, 76, 78, 80, 112–115,
    119; women's compared to men's
    19, 84, 85–86; women's networking
    events 70–71, 79–80, 115; 'wrong'
    ways to network 60, 61, 62, 72–73,
    80; *see also* strategic networking
neutrality, assumptions of 15, 63;
    see also meritocracy; rationality,
    assumptions of
New Girls' Networks 66–69, 76, 79
Nickson, D. 48, 51
nomination committees 16
non-profit boards 6
Noon, M. 101
Norway 1–2, 7–8

objectivity 24, 35, 40, 42, 44
Old Boys' networks 17, 19, 53, 69,
    75–76, 79, 92, 115, 120
one-on-one networking 74–75, 115
open-mindedness 39, 40
opinion conformity 12
opportunism 61
Opsahl, T. 7, 8, 10
Orgad, S. 82, 91, 116, 117
othering 49
over-qualification 9, 11, 12

parenting 25–26
part-time nature of non-executive
board membership 7
passivity 81, 92, 94, 106–107
patience 61–62, 82, 94–96, 99–100,
106–107, 116, 120, 126
peer sponsorship 114
personality types 12, 17, 35,
38–41
personal recommendations: from
female networks 21; lean-in
discourse 85; New Girls' Networks
66–69; opacity of appointment
process 15, 53, 112, 114–115;
strategic networking 56, 62–65,
78–79; subtle networking 59–60,
62–65, 78–79; visibility to
gatekeepers 20–21, 114–115;
see also networks
playing the game: ideal board
member 32, 51; lean-in discourse
81, 85, 86–88, 89, 105, 106, 115;
networking 65, 68, 70; privilege
119; sitting back discourse 94
portfolio careers 2, 26, 66
positive discrimination 100, 101
positivism 9
power: and corporate elites 119, 121;
and gatekeeper roles 114–115; and
headhunters 47, 86; imbalances 7,
13; and social networks 19
previous board experience 10, 30–33,
109; *see also* 'right' experience
discourse
private members' clubs 55
privilege 116–117, 118–123, 124; *see
also* elite identities
Probyn, E. 90
professional executive class 119
prospective 4–5
publicly advertised roles 16
'pulling the ladder up' 79
pushiness 59, 61, 77–79, 106–107,
113–114, 116–117, 120
Pye, A. 12, 14, 50, 110, 111, 123

qualifications 9
Queen Bees 79, 122
quotas 1–2, 8, 29, 101, 108, 117,
118, 125

radar, getting on the 54; *see also*
visibility
radical feminist theory 126

rarity/unusualness of female suitable
candidates 29
rationality, assumptions of 11, 15,
35, 42, 52, 110–112, 120; *see also*
meritocracy
reciprocity 66
recommendations: from female
networks 21; lean-in discourse
85; New Girls' Networks 66–69;
opacity of appointment process
15, 53, 112, 114–115; strategic
networking 56, 62–65, 78–79;
subtle networking 59–60, 62–65,
78–79; visibility to gatekeepers
20–21, 114–115; *see also* networks
recruitment firms *see* headhunters;
search/recruitment firms
relationship management 88
reproductive truth effects 29, 51,
67, 109
reputation, prior good 28, 53
resilience 45
respectability, norms of 13, 121–122
'right' experience discourse: and the
ideal board member 11, 24–30,
48–49, 52, 109–112; lean-in
discourse 85, 88; networks 74,
75; previous board experience
27–28, 31, 32; recommendations
64, 65; and the right fit 45;
sitting back discourse 95; wild
cards 37
'right personality' discourse 35,
38–41, 45, 49–50, 109–112
'right shamelessness' 85
rigorous appointment processes 16,
17, 18
Riley, S. C. 102, 104, 108
risk: masculine and feminine attitudes to
13; risk aversion 13, 34–35, 50, 110;
risk experience 29; of taking on new
board members 10; 'wild cards' 36
Roberts, A. 10, 13, 35, 50, 82, 110, 113
Robertson, M. 78, 112, 113
Rottenberg, C. 82, 91, 105, 115, 116
rubber chicken circuit 72

Sandberg, S. 21, 82, 117
Sapphire Partners x–xi
Sauerborn, E. 128
Savage, M. 17, 78, 119, 121, 125
Scharff, C. 118
Sealy, R. 10, 11, 14, 27, 48, 49, 118,
123, 124, 125

search/recruitment firms: appointment processes 14, 15, 16–18; and levels of relevant experience 28–29; and networks 65; sitting back discourse 91–92; strategic networking 54; 'wild cards' 35–37; *see also* headhunters

Seierstad, C. 7, 8, 10, 118, 125, 127
self-blame 88–91, 96
self-confidence 45, 91, 97, 100
self-nomination 20
self-promotion 27, 73
senior executive positions, women in 3, 121, 124
sexism 47, 103, 104, 118
sexualised language 84, 85, 122
shamelessness 59, 72–73, 84, 85, 122
shareholder interest protection 12
Sheridan, A. 6, 8, 9, 10, 12, 14, 18, 49
Shilton, J. 118
signalling (of interest) 58
Simpson, R. 111, 112
Sinclair, A. 13
sitting back discourse 82, 91–104, 106–107, 115–118
'skeletons' (lack of) 28
skills for board membership 11, 12–13, 14, 27–28
sociability 40–41
social capital 9, 19, 20, 124
social class 17, 78, 119
social constructionism 4
social justice 7, 9, 118, 126, 127
social network theories 19, 21
social relationships 55, 72, 77
socio-cultural contexts 22
solidarity between women 21, 68, 91
spatial language 58
specifications of role 16
sponsorship 21, 64, 78–79, 114–115
status quo, challenging 65, 115, 120
Stern, I. 6, 12, 16
Stokes, R. 102, 118
strategic networking: alongside subtle networking 58, 59–60, 112–115, 119; art of networking 53–56; avoiding the Handbag Society 70–71, 72, 74, 75, 77; choosiness 95; compared to subtle networking 57; lean-in discourse 89; New Girls' Networks 68–69; personal recommendations 63–64
strategic thinking 12

strong network ties 19, 113
subjective skills 12
subjectivity in appointment processes 24, 35, 38, 40–44, 77, 110, 111
subtle networking 53, 57–62, 76, 78, 80, 112–115, 119
'superwomen' 103
swelled pool 99

targets 118, 125; *see also* quotas
testosterone 13
Theranou, P. 8, 9, 19, 20
tick-box exercises 32
tokenism 21, 118
training for NED roles 74–75
transparency 16, 56, 105, 113
truth effects 29, 51, 109

utilitarianism 7

van den Brink, M. 18, 20, 21, 22, 112, 113–114, 124
visibility 18–22, 28, 53, 58, 60–62, 70–73, 83, 114
voice 14
voluntary quotas 1, 2, 8

Wang, M. 2, 8
Warhurst, C. 48, 51
weak social network ties 19
wealth elites 119
West, C. 9
Westphal, J. D. 6, 12, 16, 29, 50, 52, 111, 123
White, L. J. 10, 109
white men: fewer barriers to entry for 10; as the headhunted 17, 18; as headhunters 17; as reference 'norm' 12
wild cards 35–38
Williams, K. 17, 78
Wirz, M. 14, 16, 17, 18, 21, 51, 52, 78, 92, 110
Withers, M. 15, 16, 23n4
Witz, A. 124
women-as-saviours narrative 13
women-on-boards agenda 2, 98–104, 107, 117, 119, 124, 125–128
women-on-boards networks 21, 66, 70–77

'Women on Boards' report *see* Davies'
Review
women's networking events 70–71,
79–80, 115
women-women relationships 19–20,
21, 66–69, 91, 115, 122
word of mouth 84, 85, 93; *see also*
recommendations

working (within) the system 86–88;
see also playing the game
'wrong' experience discourse 33–35,
36–37, 103, 110

Zattoni, A. 11
Zimmerman, D. H. 9
Zorn, D. M. 10, 109

Printed in the United States
by Baker & Taylor Publisher Services